The Hungry Spirit

The Hungry Spirit

> BEYOND CAPITALISM:
> A QUEST FOR PURPOSE IN
> THE MODERN WORLD

Charles Handy

BROADWAY BOOKS
NEW YORK

BROADWAY

A hardcover edition of this book was published in 1998 by Broadway Books.

Broadway Books titles may be purchased for business or promotional use or for special sales. For information, please write to: Special Markets Department, Random House, Inc., 1540 Broadway, New York, NY 10036.

BROADWAY BOOKS and its logo, a letter B bisected on the diagonal, are trademarks of Broadway Books, a division of Random House, Inc.

First trade paperback edition published 1999.

Designed by Brian Mulligan

The Library of Congress has catalogued the hardcover edition as:

Handy, Charles B.
The hungry spirit : beyond capitalism : a quest for purpose in the modern world / by Charles Handy.
p.   cm.
Includes bibliographical references and index.
ISBN 0-7679-0187-8 (hc)
1. Capitalism—Moral and ethical aspects. 2. Values.
3. Individualism.   I. Title.
HB501.H339   1998
330.12′2—dc21   97-34273
                                                    CIP

ISBN 978-0-7679-0188-8

144915995

Contents

Acknowledgments

B OOKS WOULD never come into being if it were not for a collection of people who think that the whole enterprise is worthwhile—particularly when the author begins to doubt it. I must therefore pay tribute, once again, to my remarkable wife and partner, Elizabeth, for her continuing belief in me and for her encouragement to put as much trust in my own beliefs and experience as in the accepted orthodoxies of the time. To Kate and Scott, too, my thanks, for allowing me to use them, our children once, and now our wise friends, as occasional examples of life as it can be lived.

It is standard practice for authors to thank their publisher and editor, but for me it comes from the heart. Gail Rebuck and Paul Sidey have turned a professional relationship into one of camaraderie and true friendship. Their patience and forbearance as I struggled to make sense of the things I was trying to write about was wonderfully sustaining and their astute comments unlocked many a quandary. They have mastered the art of being helpful without seeming to be critical, and have managed to make the creation of a book a thing of pleasure rather than the long trudge that it can sometimes be. I am happy to have this opportunity to pay public tribute to them both, as well as to the team of very professional people at Random House who back them up and who seem to take as much interest in my books as I do. In America I have been touched by the warmth and enthusiasm with which the people at Broadway Books have welcomed this newcomer to their midst. I am particularly grateful to Bill Shinker and Suzanne Oaks for the care and attention which they have given me, and to all those others at Broadway who have helped to make this book a reality in America.

I have listed in the bibliography the particular authors whose work has informed this book but I realize that most of my ideas come from somewhere else, even if I am not always conscious of it. I want, therefore, to express my gratitude to all those who have educated and enriched my life, by their words or example. That includes the many students and managers in different lands who have taught me as much as or more than I taught them.

—Charles Handy
Diss, Norfolk, England

A Personal Preface

I AM WRITING these words in a room looking out over the fields and woods of East Anglia. It is an idyllic pastoral scene, just waiting for a latter-day John Constable to capture it in paint. Old photographs reveal that it looked just the same one hundred years ago. Some things don't change. In the village behind me, people fall in love, have children, walk their dogs, and gossip about their neighbors, just as they have always done. The great themes of life with which we all have to deal—love and death, loneliness and responsibility—are still with us.

Appearances can lie, however. One hundred years ago two men scythed the crop on those fields at the rate of one acre a day. Now John does the twenty acres in one day, on contract. The small farm of which those fields were a part has been swallowed up in something bigger, and a way of work has gone forever. The people in the village don't work on the land anymore, they work for computer firms, estate agents, or publishers, connected to computers and fax machines rather than the tools of agriculture. It is work that women and men do equally well, which often means that both husbands and wives are out all day. That is different. The houses have burglar alarms on their walls, when once no one here thought to lock their doors.

The alarms are there because there are more things worth stealing in those houses than there ever were before. People are better off, materially. Some, however, feel that they have missed out or, if they are young, worry that they won't ever get a chance. There are more choices about what to do, what to buy, and where to live, but that doesn't always make it easier. Although most of those houses look as if they have been there forever, the people who live in them were not born in the village and their children will leave as soon as they are qualified. It is, these days, a transient community.

Our village is a microcosm of society. At first glance, life often seems to go on much as it always did, but look more closely and change has infiltrated every part of it. Change is ingrained in life, and most of that change we would be happy to call progress. Our cottage had an outhouse when we bought it twenty years ago, and no electricity. It is much more comfortable now. Life for almost everyone in the West is more comfortable than it was. Few things, however, are unmixed blessings and the free market economic system which made it all possible is no exception.

Many of us are, I believe, confused by the world we have created for ourselves in the West. We are confused by the consequences of capitalism, whose contribution to our well-being cannot be questioned, but which divides rich from poor, consumes so much of the energies of those who work in it, and does not, it seems, always lead to a more contented world. I know of no better economic system. Nevertheless, the new fashion of turning everything into a business, even our own lives, doesn't seem to be the answer. A hospital, and my life, is more than just a business.

What good can it possibly do to pile up riches which you cannot conceivably use, and what is the point of the efficiency needed to create those riches if one third of the world's workers are now unemployed or under-employed, as the International Labor Organization (ILO) calculates? And where will it end, this passion for growth? If we go on growing at our present rate we will be buying sixteen times as much of everything in 100 years' time. Even if the world's environment can tolerate the burden, what are we going to do with all that stuff? Seventy corporations now rank bigger than many a nation state—will they grow bigger still? Does that matter?

The apparent lack of concern about these problems from those in powerful places smacks of complacency. I am disappointed by the assumption that these worries are inevitable accompaniments of change and that time, technology, and economic growth will sort most of them out. I am angered by the waste of so many people's lives, dragged down by poverty in the midst of riches. I am concerned by the absence of a more transcendent view of life and the purposes of life, and by the prevalence of the economic myth which colors all that we do. Money is the means of life and not the point of it. There must be something that we can do to restore the balance.

The fault, no doubt, is ours. We have allowed ourselves to be distracted by the false lures of certainty which are offered by the competing traditions of science, economics, and religion. Science appears to suggest that we are shaped by forces beyond our control and might as well lie back and enjoy it. Economics offers material prosperity as the only universal goal, and, if we accept that premise, all else follows ineluctably, according to the laws of the market and the dictates of efficiency. Religions, too, offer their own form of false certainty, promoting the idea that if you keep to their rules, or trust in a superior power, all will be well, if not in this world, then in some imagined other world. Reason says that any of these traditions might be right, but our hearts revolt at the thought that our purposes should be so preordained in one way or another.

Even George Soros is worried, he who has made billions by his juggling of the markets. Nowadays he puts much of his wealth into foundations designed to foster the open society in countries recently emerging from the state of closed societies, dictatorships, or totalitarian governments. In a significant article in *Atlantic Monthly* in January 1997 he expressed his concern that laissez-faire capitalism was itself creating a closed society in which only one thing counted—material success. A truly open society, he said, accepts that there is no such thing as absolute truth. A variety of beliefs must be allowed to coexist and need protection. We must all be free to make up our own minds. Open societies are demonstrably more vigorous, more prosperous, and more stimulating than closed ones. Capitalism, which was supposed to set us free, may be enslaving us in its turn, with its insistence on the dominance of the economic imperative.

No wonder we are confused, and hungry for something else. My hope stems from a hunch that many people share these doubts and worries, that they know that life is not just a business. They sense that, maybe, it is love and friendship, a responsibility for others or a belief in a cause of some sort, not money, that makes the real difference in the way life goes, that it is, in the end, important to believe in a purpose for our lives, even though it may be hard to work out what it is. Most of us have modest ambitions. We want to live decent lives in a decent society, and, given half a chance, that is what could happen because we are all of us mixtures of good and evil impulses, of heart and head in the same body. If we trusted ourselves, and our hearts, a little more, and the dogmas of the disciplines rather less, we could regain control over the things which really matter.

Nevertheless, confused as we are by economic and scientific pseudo-certainties, some clues are needed. Can capitalism be made more decent and its instrument, business, work more obviously for the good of all, everywhere? Can the wealth created be used so that all can benefit, not just the fortunate few, and can education be reinvented to give everyone a start in life and not just the clever kids? Can we look after ourselves and have a care for others as well? What rules should there be in a decent society and who should set them? What part should government play in all of this? What, ultimately, is the real purpose of life? There are no sure answers to that last question, only the one that each of us believes to be right.

Beliefs begin when the facts run out. Nobody can prove to anyone else's satisfaction that their beliefs are right. But when they click with other people's sense of what is true, they can be very powerful indeed. I suspect, in fact, that the next great clashes in the world will not be between nation states, or between conflicting economic systems, but between belief systems, which sometimes get called religions (such as Islam), sometimes civilizations (India or China), and sometimes cultures (Western). If capitalism is to be our servant rather than our master it will be because our belief systems want it that way. Beliefs are always personal but they need not be private. Shared and spread they can change the world more than governments can. It is well, therefore, that you should know how my own set of beliefs was formed, before you start to read the thoughts that arise from them.

It all started with a death, that of my father, whom I had thought a quiet and rather ordinary man, albeit kind and loving.

He was rector of a small Protestant parish in rural Ireland for forty years. He was unambitious for promotion, careful about money—careful because there wasn't much—punctilious in his work and sincere in his beliefs, which were conventionally Christian. He did not have much to do with the wealth-creating part of the world, or with its products.

By the time I was eighteen I had resolved never to be poor, never to go to church again, and never to be content with where I stood in life. I went off in search of fame and fortune, first as an oil executive in Southeast Asia, then as an economist in the city of London, ending up, by the time my father died, as a professor at the new London Business School, dashing hither and thither, the published author of papers and books, on the edge of the big time, too busy to attend to my family. "Until I was ten," said my daughter years later, "I thought you were the man who came to lunch on Sundays."

Then my father died, in the fullness of his years. I have written elsewhere about his funeral, but I was staggered by the numbers who came to say farewell to this quiet man, and the emotion which they showed. He had clearly affected the lives of hundreds of people in ways I had never imagined. He had obviously got something right which I had been too obtuse to see. And, in the end, too late for him to know, he affected my life, too.

I realized that what one believes about life, and the point of life, does matter. I had put my faith, until that moment, in success, money, and family, probably in that order. I still think these things are important, although I would now reverse the order, but I hanker after a bigger frame in which to set them. At other times, I think "Why bother?" and remember Cyril Connolly who, when asked for his definition of the good life, replied: "Writing a book, dinner for six, travelling in Italy with someone you love." That's a fairly middle-class definition of fun, and fun, however you define it, should be an important part of life, but not the whole of it. Even Cyril Connolly might have got bored with his dinner parties and his Italian journeys, not to mention the very mixed pleasure of writing a book. "We are here on earth to fart about," said Kurt Vonnegut, "don't let anyone tell you different." But, at the last count, Kurt Vonnegut had written fifteen books. That is serious work. Head and heart were pulling him in different directions, maybe . . .

My doubts and confusions are not unique. At the end of his history of the twentieth century, *The Age of Extremes*, Eric Hobsbawm concludes: "Our world risks both explosion and implosion. It must change . . . If humanity is to have a recognizable future, it cannot be by prolonging the past or the present. If we try to build the third millennium on that basis, we shall fail. And the price of failure, that is to say, the alternative to a changed society, is darkness."

What, then, *is* life about? And what is progress? In seeking to answer these questions, I am going to be covering some well-travelled ground, because philosophers have been debating these matters for at least 2,500 years. But, as one of those philosophers, Jean-Paul Sartre, pointed out, we must all still work these things out for ourselves.

Strange things are happening to our institutions. Businesses, where most people work, at one extreme are getting smaller, almost disappearing as institutions, but, at the other, are getting bigger than nation-states. At the big end, this means that they are effectively responsible or answerable to no one except themselves and those involved with them. At the other end, they no longer have the same responsibility that they used to have for those who now work with them, rather than for them, many of them outside the organization. The old idea of property as the basis for wealth and power no longer works, when the thing that organizations think that they own turns out to be us. We, the individuals, aren't ownable any more. As all the traditional structures disappear, we all inevitably become responsible for ourselves, more completely than ever before. We are "condemned to be free."

Organizations, as well as individuals, have therefore got to decide what they are about before they can decide what they have to do. A philosophy for our time is needed, both for institutions, particularly those of business, and for individuals who, thank God, are no longer the human resources of some amorphous entity but persons, each with his or her own life to lead. Yet we are not free to lead that life without regard for others. We cannot escape the connectedness of the world, not least because the more we concentrate on what we are best at, the more we will need the expertise of others. Self-sufficiency is an idle dream. Even those who cultivate their own organic plots need trucks built by others to drive their produce to market along roads maintained by others.

The meeting of self and others, of individual, or individual institution, and the community, is probably the most complex issue of our time. In the Anglo-Saxon world the individual is the starting point, but in Germany, and Japan and the Chinese subcontinent particularly, the community has traditionally come first. Both individual and community, however, have finally to meet in this modern world, in a compromise between freedom and commitment. Irishman that I am, I cannot live without others, but my life starts with me. I call it Proper Selfishness, the search for ourselves that, paradoxically, we often pursue best through our involvement with others. To be Properly Selfish is to accept a responsibility for making the most of oneself by, ultimately, finding a purpose beyond and bigger than oneself. It is the paradox of Epicureanism, that we best satisfy ourselves when we look beyond ourselves.

The argument of this book is that, in our hearts, we would all like to find a purpose bigger than ourselves because that will raise us to heights we had not dreamed of. If the individualism which is at the heart of capitalism became redefined as this sort of Proper Selfishness, society might become a better place instead of the screw-my-neighbor world it seems to be. This new individualism looks beyond materialism to something greater. The freedom and the choices which capitalism and liberal democracy make possible do not have to be squandered on yet more things, but can be used instead to liberate more people to be as well as to have. No laws can make this happen, only a release of the human spirit, which I suspect is hungry for it, waiting only for such a Proper Selfishness to be fashionable and admired.

Proper Selfishness is an optimistic philosophy because it believes that we are ultimately decent people. There is good and evil in all of us and it is only sensible for society to attempt to control the evil. But much of life is a self-fulfilling prophecy. If you think the worst of people and show it, they will often prove you right. If the systems we design are based on the principle that people cannot be trusted, then those people won't bother to be trustworthy. On the other hand, if you believe that most people are capable and can be relied upon, they will often live up to your expectations. Optimists are always prey to disappointment, but life without hope is dismal.

—Charles Handy
Diss, Norfolk, England

A Creaking Capitalism

In this first part of the book, I explore some of the puzzles and worries of the capitalist societies, societies which are not working as well as we expected them to, and which are not working for the good of all. The market, competition, and efficiency, all good things in themselves, turn out to have unintended side effects. Capitalism has proved itself superior to communism and to the more extreme varieties of socialism, but has failed, thus far, to show that it has the complete answer to our desire for progress.

The Limits of Markets

I N A F R I C A, they say that there are two hungers, the lesser hunger and the greater hunger. The lesser hunger is for the things that sustain life, the goods and services, and the money to pay for them, which we all need. The greater hunger is for an answer to the question "why?", for some understanding of what that life is for.

In the capitalist societies, however, it has been our comfortable assumption, so far, that we can best satisfy the greater hunger by appeasing the lesser hunger. It has been mightily convenient to think that better bread, and a bit of cake to go with it, would make us all content, because governments and business together might be able to deliver on that contract. The consequence of such thinking is that money ultimately becomes the measure of all things, as Karl Marx warned that it would, with the market as its handmaiden. The more competitive we can make things, the better things we will have at a better price, the richer we all will be, and the richer we are the more content we should be. We can measure our lives in dollar bills, pound notes, or deutsche marks, and then compare our scores.

THE TROUBLE WITH MONEY

Gordon Comstock, the central figure in George Orwell's 1936 novel about poverty in London, *Keep the Aspidistra Flying,* liked to adapt the chapter in the Bible that some people use at their wedding, the one from the Epistle to the Corinthians about charity, or love, to make it more apposite to the times. He replaced "charity," with "money" so that it read:

> Though I talk with the tongues of men and of angels, and have not money, I am become as a sounding brass, or a tinkling cymbal. And though I have the gift of prophecy, and understand all mysteries, and all knowledge; and though I have all faith, so that I could remove mountains, and have not money, I am nothing . . . And now abideth faith, hope, and money, these three, but the greatest of these is money.

Two generations later, including one world war and fifty years of unparalleled economic expansion, he might want to do the same. Money not only satisfies our material needs; it is also, more often than not, the measure of our success. Adam Smith rules all right, with his comforting doctrine that the pursuit of our self-interest will lead inevitably to the general good, thanks to an "invisible hand."

There is, indeed, good news in all that. We are all of us, even the poorest, much better off, in material terms, than our grandparents ever were. Money breeds creativity. Money also brings choice, and freedom of a sort. Today, anyone with any intelligence and a bit of get-up-and-go can make money. Gordon Comstock, Orwell's hero, or victim, decided to renounce money and materialism on principle, and then found life to be degrading, disgusting, and depressing. No way did the poor seem to be blessed, in his experience. Gordon settled, in the end, for a return to bourgeois values, symbolized by the aspidistra in the parlor.

Money obviously does matter, but—except to a minority, and to those who haven't got any—it doesn't matter most. Teachers don't decide to be teachers because the job will make them rich, which doesn't mean that they are happy to work for inadequate salaries or don't believe that more responsibility merits more pay. But money, however necessary, is not their scorecard of success.

At one time I taught a mixed bunch of businessmen, government workers, teachers, nurses, and voluntary workers, who were all eager to learn some of the rather dubious but fashionable theories of management. I sent them off to spend days in each others' very different organizations. The businessmen always came back amazed. "We discovered levels of motivation beyond anything we experience in our own companies, and yet these people work for peanuts." Odd. Had they never met actors, artists, teachers, or nurses before? Seemingly not.

My guess is that most of us know that there are more important things than money, as Aristotle pointed out long ago: "Wealth obviously is not the good we seek, for the sole purpose it serves is to provide the means of getting something else. So far as that goes, the ends we have already mentioned (pleasure, virtue, and honor) would have a better title to be considered the good, for they are to be desired for their own account."

We can all nod agreement to Aristotle, who has an annoying habit of pointing out the obvious, but much of the world that we live in speaks only with the language of money. Everything now has a "bottom line," even schools and voluntary organizations. Meeting our budgets is the new priority. Without money we feel impotent. All of us imagine that we could do with more of it, whether to spend, to save, or to give to others. Money has come to be the common denominator in our societies, and greater wealth the first declared aim of every government of every persuasion.

Money, too, is the only thing that counts in that league table of nations, the gross national product (GNP). If the product or the activity does not have a price it doesn't get counted. By default, the means have become the ends. Money has ended up mattering most. Or so we say, or so our politicians think we say, when they solicit our votes, on the pretext that they will put ever more of those dollar bills or pound notes into our pockets. But there is an uneasy feeling in the Western world that all is not what we say it is. We have become the prisoners of our own rhetoric, of the money myth.

Maybe, however, the greater hunger is not just an extension of the lesser hunger, but something completely different. Maybe money is a necessary but not sufficient condition of happiness, in which case, more money will not help, if you already have enough. More central heating does nothing to make you more comfortable when you are already warm enough, although everyone in a cold climate needs enough heating to operate.

That could be disturbing news for governments and economists, because it would mean that there really were limits to growth—not physical or environmental ones this time, but psychological and philosophical ones—much more difficult to deal with. How do you please the people when the promise of more and cheaper bread does not work for everyone? How can an economy grow unless most people want more bread, always and forever? More awkward still is the growing awareness that the market philosophy, the route to cheaper and better bread, and the principle at the heart of capitalism, has begun to throw up some worrying side effects.

THE TROUBLE WITH THE MARKET

Neither Adam Smith nor his successors, with a few extreme exceptions, believed that the whole of public activity should be left to the market. For one thing, a market system depends on a legal framework and a way of enforcing those laws. No one has seriously suggested that the police and the law courts should be run by private concerns for profit. Nonetheless, the recent vogue for privatization suggests that we should push the market philosophy as far as it can go. There are dangers in that approach, dangers which can distort our priorities.

Businesses live and die by the market. It is a wonderful discipline, giving out its automatic signals as to where shortages lie, or unnecessary surpluses. It is, with its built-in incentives and penalties, a spur to invention and improvement, but many do die in the process. Even big corporations seldom live longer than forty years, or deserve to. But schools, hospitals, and welfare agencies cannot be allowed to die when they are inefficient, because there might not be any others nearby to replace them. Unlike businesses, the better schools cannot expand indefinitely, or they would, in their turn, almost certainly get worse. Creating market situations for such bodies tends to mean, therefore, that the best get less good and the worse get worse. Not what was intended at all.

Forget the institutions. Think of the individuals. Markets are uninterested in products that cost more than the revenue they produce, or in customers who cost more to service than they pay. If society worked to strict market logic, those individuals whose skills were so poor that they could not add enough value through their work to cover their cost of living would be discarded. Should we then export them, or condemn them to death? The insurance principle which, either explicitly or implicitly, guarantees health care to the citizens of all the democracies should not, in strict market logic, take on as risks those who are likely to have expensive and incurable illnesses. Should AIDS sufferers therefore be refused treatment, or the old put-at-the-back-of-the-line? Unregulated, buses and trains would not run to remote outposts, or would charge so much to do so that no one could afford to use them, thereby justifying the removal of the service. Markets don't work where the human cost of failure is unacceptable.

This is not to deny the critical role of the market in any developed society. The extension of the physical reality of the town center marketplace into a key economic concept was one of the most fruitful developments in the history of civilization. But we should not be idolaters. The market has its limits, and its unintended consequences. It is only a mechanism, not a philosophy. It is clear that the disciplines of the market don't work everywhere. In particular, they don't work where the outcomes are either unpriced or unclear, and they don't work where the supply is limited or rationed.

It is not clear, for instance, how the outcome of a prison should be measured, partly because we haven't made up our minds whether the purpose of prison is to punish, to deter, or to rehabilitate the inmates. Unless and until we work out what the purpose is, we can't measure the results. Without a clear definition of desired results, any market for prison management would have to focus on the one thing that can be measured: the costs or the inputs. But competing on costs does not necessarily guarantee the best outputs. The same argument applies to most public service institutions. Where outputs cannot be measured the competition has to focus on inputs, but the cheapest hospital or school is not necessarily the best.

A limited, but desired, commodity creates the monopoly situation that all suppliers hanker for and customers fear. Some monopolies, however, cannot be avoided, usually because duplicaton or triplication of a facility, such as a pipeline, an electricity supply line, or an extra research hospital, would be unduly wasteful and expensive. The cost of the extra resources would more than outweigh any benefit to be gained from the pressures of competition. In such situations a regulatory body steps in to make sure that the facility is made available to all who want to use it at a fair price for all concerned. The market, left to itself, would not work. But regulators are not all-wise and all-knowing. They themselves have a monopoly power which is not always exercised fairly.

The difficulty lies in deciding where the market can be allowed to operate and where it would be harmful. Respect, not idolatry, is needed.

Artificial markets don't work

In the early days of Gorbachev's *perestroika*, when the first Russian managers arrived for a course at the London Business School, some of us joked that the Russians knew about costs and knew about prices, they just didn't realize that the two were connected. Thinking about it, later, I realized that this was, of course, also true of most of the things which are run by governments—hospitals, schools, government agencies, and so on.

The beauty of the market is that it connects prices with costs, which is why privatization is a good idea, but it only works if the customers know the prices and if they have a choice. Putting public utilities into the marketplace creates private monopolies until alternative suppliers arise, and an official regulator, no matter how determined or how clever, is not the same as a free choice for the customers.

At the other extreme, there are some organizations which arrange an internal competition between their different business units, with the best one getting to serve the customer. Well-intentioned though this is, it usually ends up with more bureaucracy and more ill-feelings. Any business that concentrates on its internal mechanisms more than on the customer is, ultimately, a bad business. Markets are great inventions but they work because they provide customers with a price and a choice. Leave either of these out and you end up serving the bureaucrats rather than the customer.

Markets can lower standards

The market plays to the consumer, but it is not always the case that the consumer wants or gets the best, even when the price is the same.

Bringing competition into television in Britain, with 230 channels in place of 5, will almost certainly result in a lowering of standards as more broadcasters fight for the same pool of advertising money, if America's example is anything to go by.

Unlike in America, university degrees in Britain are graded as First, Second or Third Class degrees. The understanding is that a system of mutual inspection, in which each university department is checked by its counterpart in another university, will guarantee a common standard, but the universities are competing for students and the temptation to apply less stringent standards and to award a higher number of Firsts in order to attract more and better students is strong, and, by all accounts, is not always resisted. It would be better to leave it to the market to decide, as happens in most other countries.

Even that solution does not always work. In 1967, there were two courses in Britain offering the MBA degree in Business Studies. Thirty years later there are 120. Obviously the quality must vary, but the degrees are the same. There are two markets here. The immediate market—the would-be student—wants as short a course as possible, provided it has the right cachet. The ultimate market, the employers, is not always as discriminating as it would like to be because it is largely based on hearsay. There is a temptation to compress and to massage the courses to make them more attractive to potential students, as long as this does not deter the ultimate customers.

Markets are now global

The market is now international, global even, for certain products. The idea that the invisible hand of the market would work to "the benefit of all" must therefore also be interpreted on a global basis. It may be more efficient, in market terms, and therefore more profitable, to have your airline tickets processed in India rather than London, or your cars assembled in the Czech Republic rather than Detroit. But the people who will benefit the most are the workers in India or Prague, or the shareholders in New York, while the people in London or Detroit will only benefit indirectly from some possible tax on the profits.

In Adam Smith's far simpler world, those who lost out could still share in some of the resulting benefits to the community, could at least envisage, perhaps even meet, those for whom they had been forced to make a sacrifice. It may all be a win-win game in the end, but that depends on how large you think the playing field is. The world may be too large a playing field for people to comprehend. It is asking a lot of people to work for the good of humanity at large if it has to be done at personal cost. The global market can seem a cruel place, yet protection is only a short-term device.

Markets can deepen differences

The theory is that markets force everything to a common standard. Everything catches up with the best, or the cheapest, in the end. What seems to be happening, however, is that the markets for some products—computer software, films, legal services, sports stars—are now so huge, as a result of going global, that "the winner takes all," as the title of Robert Frank and Philip Cook's book aptly puts it.

Top professionals, whether they are tennis stars, lawyers, or authors, these authors point out, can earn many multiples of the pay of people from the same stable, who are just not quite as good, or as well marketed. The bigger the market, it seems, the bigger the rewards to the really successful players, be they individuals or corporations. The business conference circuit is now an international one. Whether the venue for the event is Qatar or Sydney or Phoenix, the organizers want the same top names as speakers. Without them, they feel, the event would lack international standing, and would not attract the audience they want. These names are able to state their own price, although, in many cases, the material they deliver is no better in content or style than that which a host of less well-known experts could provide.

Marketing then becomes as important as content, but marketing is expensive, however it is done. It is hard for any newcomer to break into the circuit. Meanwhile the costs, and therefore the prices, of the events go up. In theory, higher prices will encourage new entrants with lower prices, but this market is more about prestige than reality, and prestige thrives on high prices and suspects the cut-price deal. The result is a market that seems as unreal as it is unfair.

Business conferences may one day price themselves out of existence, but not the other top professions. Who, when their life or liberty are at stake, would not pay all that they could afford for the best lawyer in town? But how do you know who is the best? Price is one good indicator. The old equation, which relates price to quality of goods delivered, then breaks down. Even if we only get 10 percent more from paying three times as much, we will take the more expensive option if we can afford it, because we want that extra 10 percent, whatever it costs.

Mega earnings to a few and peanuts to the rest is not what the markets were supposed to deliver, even if the customer seems prepared to pay for the exorbitant costs.

Markets ignore the free

Anything that is unpriced is ignored by the market. The environment is the most obvious example. Air is free, so we use it and pollute it, without penalty most of the time, likewise the oceans. What is not owned is not priced, and therefore cannot be included in any calculation. The answer, clearly, is to price these things, by taxing their use, or at least their abuse, but the practicalities of policing it are difficult.

Some things are not free, but because we don't fully price their everyday use they *seem* to be free. Roads are one example. In Britain all roads are free to all users, with the exception of a few toll bridges. They are, of course, funded from a variety of taxes on vehicles and fuel, but their use is not directly priced. We don't know what each journey costs the country, or even us.

A rail journey, where every extra mile is directly priced, seems therefore to be more expensive than the equivalent journey by road, although, when everything is taken into account, it is often the road that is more expensive. The average person is unable to make the price comparison so the market does not work. More people use the roads than they would if they knew what it really cost them. The answer would be to put roads and rail on a comparable basis, making both apparently free, or both priced per mile.

Unpriced work in the home or in the community is another obvious example of a free good ignored by the markets. Since there is no financial reward from home work, parents are tempted to take their skills into the paid labor market and to hire someone else to do what they would have had to do for nothing. It may be that there is more satisfaction in the normal job market, but one suspects that if a way was found to pay parents for their important work at home, many of those parents would want to devote more time to it.

It is true that I would not want to be paid for parenting, myself. It would demean the gift of my time and love to my children. Similarly, I don't want to be paid for the time I give to voluntary associations. It is often more pleasurable to give than to earn. On the other hand, if you live in a market it is tempting to live by the market. The things that have no price are either beyond price, like the care of one's children, or worthless, because no one seems willing to pay for them. It is not surprising, therefore, to find that most volunteering is done by those in jobs, not, as one might think, by the unemployed, the retired, the housewife or househusband. If one's labor seems worthless in the paid market, it can seem to be a gift not worth giving away in the free market.

We can't put all work into the market. Even if I wanted to be paid for parenting, who is going to pay me? What we can do is to recognize more publicly that free work makes a vital contribution to society. There is no fundamental reason why an estimate of its value could not be included in GDP statistics, since GDP stands for Gross Domestic Product. What doesn't get counted doesn't count, but market price need not be the only number that gets counted. By ignoring what is inevitably unpriced the market can distort our values.

THE TROUBLE WITH COMPETITION

If you lived alone on a desert island you wouldn't need money or markets and you wouldn't miss them. But you might find it very difficult to live without someone to compare yourself with. That is where competition comes in. It provides the basis for comparisons, so that we know what it means to be clever, or reliable, a good cook or a fast runner. It would be hard to know what these things meant if you knew no one else. Competition is, therefore, an essential part of any system, although it does not need to be measured in money to work. It sets standards.

Visiting Hungary when it was still a centrally planned economy, I inquired why they had two fertilizer plants for a relatively small country at a time when there were major economies of scale in fertilizer production. "It's simple," they said, "if there was only one plant, we in the center would have to set the standards and we don't know what fertilizers should cost. So we have two, and by competing they set their own standards."

Competition generates energy, rewards winners, and punishes losers. It is, therefore, the fuel for the economy. A competitive economy, Bill Clinton promised in 1992, would deliver "good jobs at good wages." Since then American business has improved its competitiveness dramatically. Exports grow by leaps and bounds, profits have bloomed. The U.S.A. is once again the most competitive large economy in the world, having previously lost out to Japan. It has also created a lot of new jobs, many more than the whole of Europe. Unfortunately, only half of those new jobs could be called "good" in any sense of the term. Competition means that America is getting richer, but some Americans are getting very much richer than others, and some are actually getting poorer. Productivity isn't good for everyone.

Partly for this reason, Europe has not pursued competitiveness as aggressively as America has and so has failed to create jobs. For every 100 jobs that existed in Europe in 1975 there are now only 96. In America there are 156 for every 100 in 1975. On the other hand, the gap between the richest and poorest 10 percent is twice as great in America as in Europe. The poorest 10 percent in America now earn only half the amount, in real terms, than their counterparts do in the leading European economies. You can't, it seems, have it both ways.

It is not even obvious that the fruits of competition—economic growth and riches—necessarily bring contentment. They walk faster in Japan, Taiwan, and urban America. The slowest walkers are in Indonesia. There are more suicides in the faster-growing countries, and more road rage. I remember my first economics teacher, a central European now working in America, and a winner of a Nobel prize, saying, rather wistfully, that he always preferred living in a country where the economy was in decline, because there was so much more time for lunch! The art and the theater were usually better, too. The trouble was that there wasn't the market for his work in such countries.

The story of Michael is all too familiar in the more competitive businesses.

It was a Sunday morning in executive land. Michael, a top-flight fifty-five-year-old manager with one of those corporations known only by their initials, was breakfasting late with his wife and daughters. "Your mother tells me," he said, turning to his twenty-three-year-old, "that you have been burning the candle at both ends—work all day and play all night. It won't do you any good in the end," he chided her gently.

"And what about you, Dad?" she replied. "We haven't seen much of you lately. When are *you* going to slow down?"

"In this business," he said, "it's like riding a bicycle—if you stop pedalling you fall off! But," he went on, "I'm planning to retire when I'm sixty and then we can do all the things which your mother and I have been dreaming of together. And now— once I've cleared my desk I'm going to have a game of tennis!"

Three hours later the phone rang. It was the hospital. Michael had had a massive heart attack on the tennis court and was dead by the time they got him to the hospital. His last check-up had found nothing wrong with him, except exhaustion and a touch too much cholesterol. His wife is sure that it was his work which killed him that morning.

What are we doing to ourselves? Consider these U.S. statistics:

42 percent of all workers feel "used up" by the end of the day.

69 percent would like to live a more relaxed life.

Parents spend 40 percent less time with their children than they did thirty years ago.

The rise in per capita consumption in the last twenty years is 45 percent, but the decrease in the quality of life as measured by the Index of Social Health is 51 percent.

> Only 21 percent of the young now think that they have a
> very good chance of achieving The Good Life, compared
> with 41 percent twenty years ago.

Some say that America is extreme in its workaholism and that
other countries will choose to be different, although I doubt it.
The British, for example, already work longer hours, but not
necessarily better, than every country in Europe. An astonishing
36 percent of non-manual staff work more than forty-eight hours
every week, and they are almost all managers or professionals.
It's voluntary, so the European ban on compulsory working
weeks longer than those forty-eight hours won't apply to them.

They don't all enjoy it any more than the Americans do. In a
1993 survey of managers by the Institute of Management in
Britain, 77 percent considered their hours stressful, 77 percent
worried about the effect on their family, and 74 percent about
their relationship with their partner. By 1996 it had got worse.
Stress, the Institute said, costs Britain forty million working days
a year and 10 billion dollars in health care. A study by the Massachusetts Institute of Technology calculated that depression at
work was costing America $47 billion a year, roughly the same as
heart disease.

So why do we do it? It can't be to improve our competitiveness or the British would be outperforming the Germans by
more than 10 percent, because they work that much longer.
Could it be that some actually prefer their work to the other
parts of their lives, or was Michael right in thinking that once
you relax, or slip, you'll be lost forever? Have we, in other words,
exchanged the over-comfortable cushion of the lifetime job for a
philosophy of a corporate marketplace in which you are only as
good as your last project or report, where the best will thrive and
the less good will be ejected?

Have we, perhaps unconsciously, decided that creative destruction, the principle at the heart of market capitalism, is also appropriate to its people, and that for the best to grow the rest must be neglected? Competition reaches down into the institution and demands a sort of corporate Darwinism, the survival of the fittest and the death of the rest, in the organization as well as in society as a whole.

If this is what is happening, the consequences are worrying. Leaving aside the stress which inevitably follows, but which, it could be argued, often brings out the best in people, as long as it doesn't kill them, a competitive philosophy within the firm will encourage people to look first to their own interests, and only secondly to the firm they work for. The short-term, then, will dominate their thinking while the competition for personal recognition will splinter group loyalties and make cooperation even more difficult than it already is, across functions, countries, and language.

More insidiously, people will lose their objectivity over time, as they focus more narrowly on the immediate task, losing touch with the world outside, the markets beyond their focus, and the way more ordinary mortals think and feel. Insensitivity is as bad for business as it is for relationships. "Blinkered, bigoted, and boring" was the comment by a group of friends on one of their number who was flying high in his corporation, which could have been jealousy but was more likely to be a prediction of problems to come both inside and outside his work, for who would want to live with, or work for, a boring, blinkered bigot?

It is all strangely reminiscent of Adam Smith's warning about his revolutionary idea of the division of labor and specialization, which did so much to increase prosperity and wealth. The division of labor, said Smith, drove economic prosperity but it rendered many an individual "not only incapable of relishing or bearing a part in any rational conversation, but of conceiving any generous, noble, or tender sentiment, and consequently of forming any just judgment concerning many even of the ordinary duties of private life. Of the great and extensive interest of his country he is altogether incapable of judging."

Yet it was then, and probably is now, to such people that we entrust the future of our country, because they are often the most successful.

These personal dilemmas are a direct result of competition. If capitalism is to retain its credibility in a democratic society we will have to find some way around these problems. We all need our bread, and a proper share of it, but bread alone won't do; we want something else as well. Can we have both, or does the bread get in the way of fulfillment? Just when we seem to have finally understood how to run our economies, people seem to want something more or something else. Jeffrey Smart, the famous Australian artist, who paints stark images of our industrial society, said once that there was a crisis in our idea of progress. You can see this in his paintings. Starkly beautiful, they show individuals dominated by their industrial creations—a tiny human figure in front of two huge trucks or a multicolored pile of oil drums.

Keynes, that prescient economist, warned us of the problem over seventy years ago. "Modern capitalism," he said, "is absolutely irreligious, without internal union, without much public spirit, often, though not always, mere congeries of possessors and pursuers. Such a system has to be immensely successful if it is to succeed. Today [1923], it is only moderately successful."

I would suggest that "moderately successful" could be an accurate description of capitalism today, and I say this in spite of the huge increases in material well-being that it has delivered in the seventy-odd years since Keynes made that statement. The reason is that the system has its flaws, as every system does. We can repair it here and there, but the real answer is to keep it in perspective. It is only a tool, and tools are not for worshipping.

When Efficiency
Is Ineffective

O NE CAN quarrel with the importance that is given to
money and markets in the capitalist scheme of things, but
no one, surely, would want to take issue with one of the main
results of a market economy, the efficient society. Maybe, in
searching for a purpose for our world, we could do worse than
settle for efficiency. Forget who gets the money. When things
work well it is for the good of all. Politicians ought, perhaps, to
give it a higher priority in their manifestos.

Russia has not got there yet, which makes life in that country
difficult. We asked our hotel in St. Petersburg for a telephone
number. The receptionist said that there was no telephone direc-
tory. "There are seven million people in this city," she said, "it
would obviously be impossible." In a year or two, it will be found
to be perfectly possible.

Efficiency, and the results of efficiency, are the most evident
fruits of capitalism, competition, and the market. More goods,

better services, lower prices, and more reliability give us all an easier and a better life. These fruits should more than compensate for any distortion thrown up by the system. Much of the time they do, but there is a real danger that our passion for efficiency is itself creating distortions. Unless we get efficiency in perspective we may find ourselves so busy being efficient that we forget the original purpose of the enterprise. Efficiency is not always the same as effectiveness.

E-mail and voice-mail are wonderful additions to business life, very efficient in rapid person-to-person communications. So efficient are they, in fact, that the head of one large consulting group complained the other day that her people are now spending so much time listening, reading, and responding to their incoming communications that they have ceased to think. Efficient? Yes. Effective? I'm not so sure.

Britain has re-invented America's "moviephone." Recently I discovered that I could book a cinema seat, choose the date and time I wanted, the price and location, give my telephone number and full credit card details, all by punching the keys on my telephone, have every detail confirmed back to me by a computer voice, go to the cinema that evening, put my card into a machine, and watch my ticket pop out—all done without any other human being. I was impressed by the efficiency of it all, but it took me a long time to do all that key punching, and the call was long-distance. Efficient for the cinema, undoubtedly, but it was quicker for me, and therefore more effective, when there was a human to take my call.

Still, at the end of the process, I did get what I wanted. Too many times when I ring a hospital or a business and am asked to press this or press that, I find neither an answer to my query, nor even a human voice. One day, I imagine, we won't go to the doctor but will only interact with the surgery computer. In Britain the government decided that it would be more efficient to pay all unemployment benefits by check and so reduce the number of visits an unemployed youngster needs to make to the welfare office, but by removing the personal encounter it lessened the pressure on the youngster to get up and going. All these interactions would be more effective if they were allowed to be less efficient.

In theory, and in due time, the market or good management should correct such flaws, but if the whole world is going down the same path to cost efficiency the consumer often has no choice and therefore no voice. These flaws are, however, merely the irritants of the efficient society, in a world where software and telephones are cheaper, more reliable, and less trouble than humans. There are more serious consequences of our love affair with efficiency.

THE THREE EFFICIENCIES

Efficiency isn't always what we think it is. In a perceptive analysis, *Everything for Sale: The Virtues and Limits of Markets*, the economics writer Robert Kuttner points out that there are three very different types of efficiency. He calls them Smithian, Keynesian, and Schumpeterian, after those three very different but influential economists. For the most part, when we talk about efficiency we are discussing the use of price to ensure that the right things are made in the right place at the right cost. This is the efficiency of Adam Smith. It is the one we are all familiar with.

But there is also Keynesian efficiency, which addresses the potential output that is lost when the economy is performing well below its full employment potential. More Adam Smith efficiency in that case does not help. It may even hurt, by driving more people out of work in order to increase local efficiencies. World War II, in America, violated most of the precepts of Adam Smith's efficiency, and allowed firms to make some indecent profits, but it pushed up GDP by 50 percent in four years and force-fed the two decades of growth that followed. Economists want to set these two types of efficiency up against each other as rival theories, when what is really lacking is a conceptual framework that allows them to co-exist.

Add in Schumpeterian efficiency and it gets even more complicated. Joseph Schumpeter preached technology as the engine of growth, but he also pointed out that to invest in technology there had to be spare resources and long time horizons. Too much Adam Smith efficiency narrows those margins, and shareholders tend to want their money sooner rather than later, leaving too little money available in the business for technological advance. Perfect competition can be mutually ruinous as everyone bids one another down in an attempt to be more cost efficient and cheaper. You need deep pockets to keep ahead of the field.

We can all recognize Schumpeterian efficiency at work if we consider creativity. Creativity needs a bit of untidiness. Make everything too neat and tidy and there is no room for experiment. Keep a tight rein on costs and there is no cash available to try new things or new ways. Cram your days too full and it's hard to find time to think. We all need a bit of slack to give us the space to experiment. Schumpeter would have understood the consultancy manager's complaint that her people had no time for thinking.

The German *mittelstander,* or small family businesses, are well known for resisting price competition, preferring to keep prices high and use their margins to invest in technological leadership.

Japan practices price competition in the export field, but also non-price competition in her domestic market, and managed, until recently, to grow four times as fast as America. It is a mistake, therefore, to assume that a competitive price is the only determinant of market success. It can be one way, instead, of pricing oneself too low and out of contention in the future. Douglass North, the first historian to win a Nobel prize in economics, observed, in his acceptance lecture, that it was what he called adaptive rather than allocative efficiency that was the key to long-term growth. Adaptive efficiency is Schumpeter's efficiency. Schumpeter beats Smith in the long run. Quality can matter more than price, but quality costs money to start with.

Finding the judicious balance among the three types of efficiency is a key task not only for managers but also for government, who can switch that balance by tax and monopoly legislation, and by regulation. If we stick to allocative efficiency alone, Adam Smith's variety, we are favored with low prices but are also likely to be stuck with low growth, high unemployment, and in the end, higher prices when we have to buy in what we failed to create. Markets need countervailing mechanisms if the costs of that sort of efficiency are not going to outweigh the benefits.

Take, for instance, the labor market. Left to itself, Adam Smith's type of efficiency drives down wages and payroll numbers but increases inequality. Worse, this competition for efficiency leaves no spare resources for the investment needed to redeem the situation by training and re-education. The incompetent are left to get more incompetent. Some form of buffer, be it a minimum wage, a learning bank, stronger unions, or legally required expenditure on training, is needed if the bottom group is not to be lost forever. It is the old analogy, that brakes allow the car to go faster.

It is not that one type of efficiency is better than the others, but that all three are relevant. If we want to boost demand we may need first to stimulate it by putting more people to work, even if that violates the Adam Smith type of efficiency. To get away with the increased costs that result, you either have to put barriers around the industries involved so that they are protected from foreign competitors, or do it only in the non-competitive parts of the economy such as the public sector. To stimulate investment in new technology we may need to discriminate against large dividends by taxing them or prohibiting them. Kuttner's analysis reminds us that it is not always heresy to suggest such things.

DUMPING THE DIRT

When Japanese manufacturers developed their just-in-time procedures they were delighted by the reduced costs of warehousing, because stocks were now, in practice, warehoused in the delivery vehicles carrying them to their factories. But those trucks soon jammed the highways around the cities, impoverishing life for ordinary citizens and requiring more and better roads, paid for by the general public. The manufacturers had dumped the costs of their improvements onto the general public.

Hospitals can improve their efficiency by discharging patients earlier, but someone still has to care for them at home. Businesses can, and do, work their staffs longer and harder, with consequent gains in efficiency within the firm, but with uncounted problems of stress and damaged relationships outside. Schools can improve their results by selecting only bright youngsters as their students, but someone else has to educate the others, or deal with the consequences of an underclass of the uneducated. Anyone can boost the short-term profits of a business by cutting out all varieties of development expenditure and slashing the staff numbers, but no one counts the human costs to those affected.

In theory, all the on-costs can be charged back to the originator. Pollution could be put on the company bill, as could human stress, or unemployment. The hospital could be asked to pay for the care in the community or at home, and the school to make a contribution to the education of the children it does not take. In practice, of course, this does not happen. Efficiency calculations are ring-fenced, confined to the economics of the particular unit; they are local and partial, which leaves society in general to pay for the unintended outcomes.

This is the necessary price, some would say, for the benefits of economic growth. There is, however, no one place where the overall costs of increased efficiency are measured against its benefits. Until the costs really hurt, efficiency is allowed its head within each unit of society, irrespective of its effects on others. The hope is that individual self-interest will ultimately result in a collective benefit, but it makes for a bumpy ride. As Adam Smith pointed out long ago, self-interest has to be balanced by what he called "sympathy," if it is to be tolerable to the rest of us. But there is, unfortunately, no way of putting sympathy into the efficiency numbers.

THE TILTING SOCIETY

John Kennedy's assumption, that a rising tide raised all boats, has turned out to be false. Even if all the boats shift a little, some rise dramatically higher than others. The pursuit of efficiency tilts society towards the few and away from the many. In an information age one can grow richer without growing much bigger, meaning that more wealth in the country no longer automatically creates more jobs. In fact, to grow at an average of, say 3 percent per annum, a society has to improve its efficiency at, maybe, 5 percent overall in order to remain competitive with the global competition.

The difference between those two numbers is disappearing jobs. In effect, to grow richer a country has, actually, to watch its corporations grow smaller. Downsizing is not a one-off phenomenon. But this drive for efficiency may erode the very civilization it is designed to promote, because its benefits do not fall equally, nor do its costs. The 20/80 formula is a familiar one in business, meaning that 20 percent of your products, more often than not, generate 80 percent of your profits. It is a formula that seems to be becoming applicable to the market society: 20 percent of the people seem to be generating, and getting, 80 percent of the extra wealth.

A competitive business soon discards the 80 percent of less profitable products, or clients, to concentrate on the better 20 percent. Much as some people might like to, society cannot jettison its less productive people in the same way, but it does not quite know what to do with them, except to keep them in limbo, offer them some rather short educational ladders, and hope that they will start to climb up them.

Forget the 20/80 society, it could be worse. The following numbers were compiled by David Korten for his book *When Corporations Rule the World:*

— In 1989 the top 1 percent of Americans earned an average of $559,795 each, receiving, as a group, more than all the bottom 40 percent.

— In 1992 the top 1000 CEOs in America received, on

average, 157 times as much salary as the average worker.

— *Forbes'* top 400 richest people had a net worth, in 1993, of $328 billion, equal to the combined GNP of India, Bangladesh, Nepal, and Sri Lanka.

— 70 percent of world trade is managed by 500 corporations.

A society in which the top 1 percent earn more, collectively, than the bottom 40 percent will not long be tolerated in a democratic state. The 40 percent will, eventually, revolt, and dictatorship, one hopes, is not an option in our societies—yet.

Britain is little different. In November 1996, a Sunday newspaper produced a chart comparing the gross weekly earnings of selected occupations and key individuals. A footnote said "the scale has been compressed at the top end to accommodate the highest earners; otherwise we would have needed 1,400 pages."

In 1996, Britain was boasting of being the fastest growing major economy in the European Union but that year it was revealed that, in 1993, 17.2 percent of British families were living below the poverty line, defined as being half of the average income for the country as a whole. This figure was up from 14.3 percent ten years before. The 17.2 percent figure compared with 5 percent in the Benelux countries, and was higher than every other country except the four most deprived states in Europe: Spain, Portugal, Greece, and Ireland. If the price of national efficiency is relative poverty for more, the more may not want it.

Francis Fukuyama, the author of *The End of History*, argued that the combination of liberal democracy and the free market was an unbeatable combination. In that sense it was the end of the historical search for perfection. It seems, however, that democracy and markets are not natural bedfellows after all. We shall either have to restrain the free market or limit democracy, unless we change our value system. Estonia, a country that is reinventing itself after forty-five years under Soviet rule and Soviet economics, is an interesting test case.

The Estonian Case

Estonia is not a name that will ring bells with everyone, but exciting things are happening there. A small country on the edge of Russia, up on the Baltic coast, it has a population of only one and a half million and is smaller than New York State. It also has a capital city, Tallinn, that is, if anything, more beautiful than Prague. But the real reason to go there, as I did recently, is to see what they are doing with their newly-discovered capitalism.

The place is buzzing. They told me that there were more Mercedes cars per head than in neighboring Finland, and more mobile phones. I could well believe it, watching the Estonian yuppies doing business in the traffic jams. Everyone we met was young, and running something—either a part of the government or one of the countless new service or information businesses that have sprung up in the five years since they broke free from the Soviet Union. And it was all remarkably efficient. If you want to see how capitalism and the free market can release adrenaline, go to Tallinn.

It must be great fun to build a country from almost nothing, particularly when it's so small that most of the people running things went to the same school. But outside Tallinn, and that cozy group of insiders, things aren't quite so rosy. Inflation is still hovering around 25 percent per annum, which is not good news for the pensioners, the small farmers, and the many people, like teachers, still on the government payroll. The small towns are still desolate places, unlit, unloved and, I suspect, unheated.

Estonia has a wonderful chance to prove that its newfound capitalism and efficiency could be to the benefit of all, not just for the educated and entrepreneurial few. Estonia could even show the rest of us how to do it, but there were all the signs that it was going to end up as yet another 20/80 society, leaving the 80 percent wondering what economic growth meant. The 20 percent were also discovering that efficiency in practice meant long hours. They were exciting hours, it was true, but they were not hours spent with the family, any more than they are in other countries. Most of the people we met were divorced.

If this exciting experiment in capitalism is to succeed, those Mercedes owners must not keep all their new wealth to themselves. They must have that "sympathy" for their fellow citizens, which Adam Smith, their new hero, insisted on, and they must be happy to invest in the future of other peoples' children as well as their own. If not, their new democracy might not long tolerate their new capitalism. Since that visit the Prime Minister has resigned, accused, although he denies it, of enriching himself at the public expense.

THE D.I.Y. ECONOMY

There is also, however, a positive side to the improved efficiency of an economy, even if it is tilted. A 3 percent annual growth rate does mean that there is 3 percent more money to spend. There may be fewer corporate jobs, but there are more potential clients and customers. There is no limit, in theory, to the numbers of services and products that could be sold to them, although it will tend to be individuals and tiny firms, rather than the new lean

corporations, that do the selling. New jobs come from new businesses, which often start as one-person operations. If we think
"customers" not "jobs," and nudge ourselves towards a self-employment society, there would be potential work for everyone.
People with money but no time are ready meat for those with
time but no money, as long as they have something useful to
offer, whether it be financial advice or walking the dog.

The "something useful" can be more exotic or quixotic. Two
examples:

I met a nurse from Cambridge, Massachusetts. "What sort of
nursing do you do?" I asked her.

She beamed. "I specialize in twins," she said, "training their
parents in the ways to look after them in the first months after
birth. I don't do triplets." she emphasized, "only twins."

"That must be a rather small niche market," I suggested.

"Oh no. You see, Cambridge, Massachusetts, has a large number of dual-career professional couples. They tend to postpone
having children until they are both in their late thirties or early
forties. They need fertility drugs to help them conceive, so they
often end up with multiple births. Then they need help, but
they've got money and are prepared to pay well for the sort of
service I provide. There's so much demand that I only do twins."

The son of a friend is twenty-eight and living in London. A
couple of years ago he met up with some young people from
Australia and New Zealand. Young people from these countries
commonly come to Europe for six months or so at the end of
their education before going back home and settling down. They
get jobs in London and tax is quite properly deducted from their
pay. When they return to their home countries, however, they
are entitled to most of that tax back, because their income in the
year as a whole seldom goes over the tax threshold. It's too complicated to reclaim it so they go home and forget about it. My

friend's son offered to reclaim the tax for them, provided he could keep 30 percent of whatever he got back from the UK's equivalent of the IRS. He now has a thriving little service business, run from his bedroom, collecting overpaid tax for occasional workers, with the full help and cooperation of officialdom.

All you need is an eye for a customer, the market, and a useful skill, be it nursing, computing, or just a willingness to help. In the service sector, you don't need much money up front. My daughter ran her first business from her pager, without an office at all.

The trouble is that those who will have to be the new self-employed and the new business starters are those who are, on the whole, the least well-equipped for it. They are the ones who have just been dismissed from their jobs, if they ever had them. They are the discards of the efficient society. It will require a major change of mindset, and a huge investment in education and reskilling, to create the sort of self-employment economy which, alone, might turn efficiency to universal advantage.

It is, therefore, worrying that only 6 percent of Americans are, officially, self-employed, half the percentage of Britons, for instance, or of Japanese. Most Americans have yet to be weaned away from the organization society, with its promise of health insurance and pension plans, however illusory these promises may turn out to be in the end. Sympathy would have to extend to paying extra taxes to make the weaning happen. In Britain, the Prince's Youth Business Trust acts as a venture capital resource for young people, providing these youngsters with start-up money and mentors from the business community to help them set up their own new businesses. More organizations like the Trust are needed if we are to change the culture, so that more people think "customers" instead of "jobs."

A CHINDOGU WORLD

Efficiency generates growth, even if that growth does not get spread around as evenly as one would like. We must, however, wonder what all that extra money will be spent on. A 3 percent growth rate continued for one hundred years would mean that we would be consuming sixteen times as much stuff as we do today. If the population remains stable, or falls, as seems most likely, the results are mind-boggling. We cannot—can we?—buy sixteen times as many cars or television sets, travel, all of us, sixteen times as far or as often, eat sixteen times as much food, or consume that amount of extra oil and gas. There will, undoubtedly, be all sorts of new goods and services but they will, increasingly, tend to be "chindogu."

What is chindogu, you may well ask. Chindogu is a Japanese word for all the useless things we might be tempted to buy—windshield wipers for your spectacles, in case you go out in the rain, slippers with mops underneath so that you can polish the floor as you walk around the house. I have all those ties that I'm never going to use—chindogu. We get a lot of it wrapped up in fancy papers every Christmas—and ever more ingenious chindogu catalogues come through my door with each day's mail. On February 14, St. Valentine's Day, Americans are expected to buy thirty million heart-shaped boxes of chocolates.

Chindogu can get exotic. A friend of mine visiting someone in Brazil found that he had six fridges in his house, five of them not plugged in. Why? he asked. Well, the Brazilian explained, when inflation was at its height there, money disappeared very quickly, like milk in the sun, so as soon as he had any cash he went out and spent it. The only things he could find that he fancied were fridges—so, chindogu fridges. Is this what "buoyant consumer demand" really means? Is this what we are all working so hard for?

Technology thrives on chindogu. Washing machines now come with twelve different programs, but most of them are never used. I can program the VCR for a month or more ahead, but I have never felt the need to test it. I bought it because it had more options than any other. I had fallen prey to the chindogu bug and had lumbered myself with a bundle of useless options. My son's new computer has features that weren't thought of when I bought my last one, two years ago. The instinct to have what he has is strong, although my reason tells me that the extra features are quite unnecessary for my needs.

I hate to say it, but many books are chindogu items. In 1995, 62,039 new titles were published in the United States alone. Presumably they each sold enough copies to keep the publishers, at least, reasonably happy, but many of them were almost certainly never read, just put on the shelf. Useless bits of processed trees. To cope with the unread books and all the other chindogu, every society has to become a throwaway economy. Otherwise there would literally be no room for it all. Waste collection and recycling become boom industries, thrift shops thrive, while postal services carry ever more catalogues and free offers. The chindogu world is a busy one.

A chindogu society may chalk up good economic numbers but it would not, on the face of it, provide good enough reasons for working or living. If "buoyant consumer demand" means a world full of junk, it is hard to see why we should want to work so hard for it. As Adam Smith also said, "No patriot or man of feeling could oppose it [growth], but the nature of this growth . . . is that it is at once undirected and infinitely self-generating in the endless demand for all the useless things in the world." He was in favor of "cultivation" as the purpose of society, but, unfortunately, he suggested no way of building that concept into the efficiency formula.

The British economist, the late Fred Hirsch, took the view that economic growth was ultimately self-limiting because that growth would increasingly come from "positional goods," things that set us apart from the neighbors—second homes with open views, membership of exclusive clubs, rare antiques. These goods were, by definition, limited because if everyone had them they would lose their exclusive value. He may have underestimated our capacity to think up new fashions and new haunts, but, again, a society fuelled mainly by envy of your neighbor is not one that seems worth fighting for, or one that many would want to live in, because there would never be any end to invidious comparisons, or to a feeling of perpetual dissatisfaction. Economic growth, fuelled by efficiency, may not, therefore, be limitless, odd though this may seem today. On the other hand, inefficiency is not an option, either, if we want a society that works.

Efficiency, one has to conclude, may be essential for the continued existence of a society, but ultimately it, and the economic model it belongs to, cannot lead to an answer to the greater hunger, the reason for living. We will need, perhaps, to create more activity outside the purely economic sphere, where the motivation will be unconnected with efficiency and more to do with intrinsic satisfaction and worth. In which case, money and the market would be marginal considerations in one's scheme of things.

At least three of my more mature friends, that is, friends of my age, have taken up the piano, a notoriously difficult instrument to learn, particularly when one's fingers are stiffening at the joints (and the ability to coordinate the different movements of two hands is known to decline with age). All three speak in glowing terms of the satisfaction they feel when they can make a piece of music sound roughly as it was meant to sound. It would be much more efficient to buy a CD, better results, less time, and probably less money—but it would have far less meaning for them. Not effective, in other words.

The same, of course, goes for all the things that so many of the British spend their time on, and which we belittle as hobbies. The seven hundred people of the country village where we spend much of our time enjoy, between them, over twenty interest groups ranging from the cricket team to the drama group to the silver thread group to the church bellringers. They are "organized around their enthusiasms," as one book on voluntary organizations once put it. The efficiency of some of these groups is often in doubt, but that is hardly the point. Sometimes the members positively glory in the communal chaos.

There is nothing new or surprising here. Many people, perhaps even most people, have always found their meaning and their satisfaction in life from activities that are quite outside the market, and far removed from any concern with efficiency. Sadly, however, what we do in private does not seem to count in public. We need to find ways to make it count, because we could then begin to escape from the myth we have made for ourselves, that only the things with a price are worth having or doing. We know that is not true. We should celebrate the fact.

THE COLLAPSE OF THE WEST

Pierre Thuillier, a French philosopher and science historian, in his book *The Great Implosion: A Report on the Collapse of the*

West, 1999–2002, has conjured up a report in 2081 by a group of historians, humanists, and poets (notably excluding scientists and economists) on the conditions that underlay the upheavals of Western society at the start of the new millennium. They pose the question: why did the elites at that time not see the writing on the wall?

The group is astonished at how the elites seemed to continue merrily on their way:

> . . . despite the most grotesque manifestations of the cult of Progress, the excesses of technocratic management, the kind of paranoia which was so evident among the so-called informational/organizational elites, the unbridled imperialism of the economic and financial institutions, the obsessive research into mechanization and automation, the regressive aspects of Western rationalism and the science which was an integral part of it, the incapacity of the governing bodies (in both industry and the State) to conduct the enterprises for which they were responsible in a humane way, the lack of imagination, sensitivity and human warmth that finally characterized the activities of all political parties, the alarming rise of individualism, the lures of the "information and communication culture" so touted by diverse sociologists and media experts, the exacerbation of the North/South imbalances, and the risks of explosion or implosion caused by the increasing numbers of the marginalized.

The fictional group is puzzled by the fact that ordinary citizens were so accepting of what was going on, grumbling when their material interests were affected but seemingly accepting the spiritual poverty so characteristic of modernity. "While much time and effort went into the material manipulation of *things,* people seemed incapable of facing fundamental questions concerning the meaning of human life." The group concluded, not surprisingly considering its membership, that the West collapsed because it no longer had any culture and had lost all its sense of poetry, for "a society is not really a society unless it is able to invent ideal concepts and myths that mobilize individual energies and bind people's souls together."

The book, published in 1996, was ignored by the French press, proving the author's point that the elites were unconcerned. The journal *Le Monde Diplomatique* was the exception, commenting in its editorial on the growing pessimism in France, where 80 percent no longer believed in the improvement of the economy:

> The discontented of last December's revolt are now being joined massively by the middle classes, who have been struck in full force by rising taxes and who see their children, in turn, being hit by unemployment, while they fear for their pension . . . The country is losing confidence in the elites, too often guilty of corruption, embezzlement, and using their influence for trafficking. There is a strong hostility towards the technostructure—all the more so since it is being held responsible, together with the government, for the social tragedy.

Ironically, the economy in France *is* improving, but nobody seems to feel better for it, or even to believe the statistics. What is true of France is also true of Britain and of much of the rest of the efficent society. The combination of impending drama and apathetic silence is eerie. For all its benefits, efficiency alone is not the answer.

The Baby in the Bathwater

M ARKETS AND efficiency have their flaws, but we must be careful not to lose the baby of capitalism in the messy bathwater of its unintended outcomes. We have, thus far, glossed over the benefits of both markets and efficiency. It is necessary to correct the balance, because if we were to abandon our belief in either we might end up substituting material poverty for the spiritual poverty that many sense today.

THE WORLD OF THE DAVOS MAN

In early February each year one thousand businessmen, financiers, officials, and intellectuals gather at the Swiss ski resort of Davos for the annual meeting of the World Economic Forum. It is the biggest business conference of the year, and the most expensive. Forty or so heads of state will also be there, living evidence that business and economics have a large part to play in politics. The businessmen, and the rather fewer businesswomen, do not go there to butter up the politicians; it is the other way round. The heads of state step up to the podium in turn to proclaim the virtues of their countries and to invite investment. Bill Gates attracts more interest in Davos than any prime minister or president.

Some people find the gloss and glitter of Davos Man hard to take. As even *The Economist* admitted, there is something uncultured about all that money-grubbing and managerialism. Profits, not poetry, are what fascinate these people, at least in their official capacities. Yet, in their enthusiasms for markets, whatever and wherever they may be, these people may do more to promote peace and prosperity than any number of well-intentioned diplomats. As never before, economic activity spills across borders, unconcerned whether the land on the other side is Muslim, Buddhist, or Western. Any service that can be digitized and transmitted—computer programming, banking services, back-office operations—can be produced and sold everywhere. This spreads commercial activity, allowing the growing populations of the developing world to have some hope of participating in the world economy and to find their future in prosperity rather than warfare. Because commerce requires continuity and predictability, it promotes order, and because that order brings prosperity there is little popular enthusiasm for disturbing it.

McKinsey, the consulting firm, estimates that the speed of data transmission will increase by a factor of forty-five between now and 2005. Whole new industries will spring from the improved communications that result. One possiblity is the privacy-management business. We will all be bombarded by so many electronic services that we will pay for "gatekeepers" to sort out some of the stuff for us. That service can be provided, electronically, from anywhere on earth, as can many other services. One shopping mall in Britain reputedly employs a Nigerian company to monitor its security videos, utilizing the fact that Nigeria is in the same time zone as Britain and has much cheaper labor.

By plausible assumptions, the world output of goods and services could easily double by 2020 while the population should increase by one third. Average living standards would then rise by two thirds. Even if a lot of the growth is chindogu it still brings more money to more people. In the process the rich countries do lose some jobs and industries to poorer countries but those countries get richer in their turn, whereupon they import from the rich, more than making up for the incomes they stole. Ultimately the costs of the new economies draw level with the old economies. Nothing stands still. Singaporeans are now proud that their standard of living is equal to Britain's and even boast that they will soon be more expensive but, of course, they add, more efficient.

Davos Man would have to accept that there are some snags along the way to this universal peace and prosperity. China's reinvigorated appetite will take some satisfying in the form of raw materials. All China's new cars will help to double her demand for oil by 2010, requiring her to import some three billion barrels a day—from somewhere. Then there is all that extra pollution those cars will bring, and the damage to the ozone layer from her new refrigerators. The same is true of the other developing countries, for growth in these lands is not environmentally neutral and raw materials are not elastic. We have been here before, however. In the 1970s "limits to growth" was the standard worry. The rundown of resources which they forecast did not come to pass then, and Davos Man's hope is that the threat will disappear this time too; that higher prices will bring forth new sources of supply and will cause people to use what they have more efficiently.

The greatest obstacle to the dream of universal prosperity is political. The new commercial opportunities will not fall equally. Can China hold itself together when parts of that country are growing at rates of 20 percent or more and others are still locked into peasant economies, or will China revert to feudal wars under warlords, in line with her past? There are new signs of economic nationalism as countries and regions are tempted by protectionism when times get difficult. When that happens, who knows whether the new wealth may not be spent on arms to fight our economic enemies? The hope, and in many ways the purpose, of the Davos meetings is that countries will continue to see the sense in cooperation for the sake of mutual prosperity. But it remains a hope, not a guarantee.

The Creativity Factory

In my thirties, I lived for a while in the United States. I was studying at the Sloan School of the Massachusetts Institute of Technology, a place too proud to call itself a university, where technology and business have always been intertwined. Over dinner with some friends one night we got to speculating on the kind of products and services the new technologies would throw up and the ones that we ourselves would back. It was a fun game and I went to bed with a mind still buzzing after a stimulating evening.

The next morning, however, it was back to work. I had put the conversation of the previous evening out of my mind when the phone rang. "It's Jack," the voice said. "You know that idea you were so enthusiastic about last night?" With some effort I switched my mind back to the dinner and worked out what he was talking about. "Well," he went on, without waiting for me, "I've called my banker and we can get the financing, so what do you say—when shall we start?"

For me, too English by half, I suspect, the evening's talk had been just that, talk. Yet to my American friend it was the opening up of a market opportunity, one, moreover, that the availability of venture capital turned into a real possibility. We didn't start a business. My academic work was too important to me to give up. Ironically, however, I learned more from that one incident than from most of my more formal studies. I learned that markets give wings to ideas.

We all dream dreams, but few of us do anything about them. On the surface it is the thought of profits that is the spur to a practical creativity, but the chance to make our dreams come true is at least as important as the profits we might make from them. It is, however, the possibility of profits that makes capital available and it is available capital that makes the difference between talk and action. In a regulated and controlled world there is little scope and even less incentive to be creative in work because there is no cash around to make it possible for dreams to come true. Better then to do what one has to do at work and keep the creativity for spare time.

The German economic miracle after the Second World War is usually attributed to the then Minister of Economics and later chancellor, Ludwig Erhard, but, as Neal Ascherson has revealed, it was the two economic officials who then presided over the joint British and American zones of occupation who were really responsible. Their names were Karl Bode, an American, and E.F. Schumacher, later to become famous as the author of *Small Is Beautiful*. Under the Occupation Powers everything initially was tightly controlled, rationed, and nationalized. There was much activity and confusion but not a lot of movement. Then Bode, said Schumacher, "came to me one day with the splendid idea that these controls ought to be scrapped, 'so let's take the handle off the controls.' " They did just that and let Erhard claim the credit for the explosion of energy and creativity that followed.

Silicon Valley in California is the ultimate creativity factory. Unlike bankers elsewhere, those in Silicon Valley bet on future possibilities rather than present assets. If you have a dream, and an idea as to how to make it happen, you will almost certainly be able to find someone to back it if it is halfway practical. Nor are mistakes fatal. Bankruptcy is not failure in the Valley but a sign of maturity. We all make mistakes, they say, but that should never stop one from dreaming. Is money the spur to all the creativity and energy? Up to a point, probably. But after that point it has to be something else. "I sold the boat and the beach apartment last week," one Valley entrepreneur told me. "I realized that I had not gone near either of them in the past year—too busy with the business." Dreams are more important than the money they bring.

It is every government's desire to create its own Silicon Valleys. They will never succeed if they try to plan and control the whole process. It is the opportunities that the market forces throw up, and the sources of money to back the dreams, that are the necessary preconditions for any creativity. Remove the market and there will be little incentive for the bankers and therefore no seed money for the entrepreneur to build his or her dream on.

For all its imperfections, the market remains the essential precondition of economic growth and development. More than that, it offers to each of us a way to express ourselves, because we all need our customers to reassure us that we are making a difference, are needed or wanted, appreciated or respected. If I could not sell my books to willing buyers I doubt that I would want to write. And if I could not find a publisher to back me the dream would go sour. Those potential buyers are the market whose promise prods the publisher's support and whose satisfaction, if it comes, is my reward.

IT'S THE ECONOMY, STUPID

This slogan was the Clinton campaign's reminder to themselves in the 1992 presidential elections in America, repeated, more gleefully, in 1996. The Democrats won both times, suggesting that voters are prepared to overlook all the disadvantages of capitalism, provided that it works.

It is possible, however, that voters take a more restricted view of the role of government than politicians do. Voters can understand that the prime responsibilities of government are to defend the nation against its enemies, and to provide a sound and stable economic infrastructure along with the necessary rules and regulations for an orderly market. After that it's up to us and our local communities, thank you very much. A sound and stable economic infrastructure typically means low inflation, a stable currency with moderate government expenditure and borrowing, resulting in moderate taxes and low interest rates. That is what voters want governments to provide and they will vote for those who they think can deliver it.

This does not mean that economics is the only thing on people's minds. It means that they sensibly see that if the playing field isn't properly prepared and tended it's hard to get on with the game of life. There is a lot more to life than economics but most of the rest should not be the concern of central government. We should not be surprised, therefore, if foreign policy and economics dominate electioneering, but we should never imagine that elections have much to do with the meaning of life.

THE PROPER PLACE OF CAPITALISM

Capitalism, then, would revert to its proper role, as a philosophy designed to deliver the means but not necessarily the point of life. Such a redefinition would allow it to avoid the frequent criticism that communism had a cause that worked for all—namely the liberation from poverty, the certainty of work, and a home for everyone—but no mechanism to deliver it, while capitalism had the mechanism, but a cause that worked only for a few. The redefinition would make it clear that capitalism is only a mechanism, one that leaves the cause to be determined by individuals for themselves. It is a liberating not a defining creed, money as the means but not the end.

Michael Novak, the American theologian and philosopher, writes eloquently and persuasively about business and morality and sees no necessary incompatibility between the two. In his book *Business as a Calling,* he sets out some very pragmatic reasons for preferring capitalism to any other alternative systems yet invented. They include the following:

1. Capitalism helps the poor to escape from poverty. Not all do, of course, but the evidence is that even at the bottom levels of American society there is a lot of churning. People don't stay at that level forever or even for a year. The unemployment figures are a snapshot at a point in time. Even if the percentage is the same one year later it will not be made of the same people. The American dream—that

everyone can be rich—is still working, unlike the more stagnant societies of North Korea, for example, or Cuba. The Soviet Union had more scientists and technical experts than most of the rest of the world put together, but all that brainpower did not make their people rich.

2. Capitalism is a spur to democracy. Not all capitalist countries are democratic but the empirical evidence is that a growing middle class, and an increasingly prosperous one, will demand more say in the government of their country and more personal liberty. The middle class, says Novak, has always been the seedbed of the republican spirit. It was the growing prosperity of Spain's middle class that ended Franco's dictatorship. China is probably on an irreversible path to a fuller democracy even though it may take a generation or more before the bulk of the non-urban population are enriched by the market system. Already, in the cities, one can sense the pressures for more personal liberties, pressures that are currently taken care of by the new freedoms to earn more and buy more but which will one day turn into demands for more political liberty.

3. Capitalism requires the rule of law, a respect for property and the rights of the individual, and necessitates a limited role for government. Capitalism is, therefore, a guarantee of stability and natural liberty, even if there are those who exploit the liberty and disturb the stability. An open economy with many individual parts has a much better chance of coping with the unforeseen than a centrally-planned authority, no matter how benign. No man is all-wise. Better therefore to let a thousand flowers bloom than to pick the favorites and water only them.

4. Capitalism reduces envy. Novak quotes Montesquieu:

"Commerce is the cure for the most destructive prejudices; for it is almost a general rule, that wherever we find agreeable manners, there commerce flourishes." To me there is a paradox in that capitalism thrives on envy as we aim to emulate or even do better than our neighbors, but at the same time gives us the opportunity to do something about it. We can choose to compete or we can choose to be different. Novak argues, therefore, that capitalism prevents the tyranny of the majority, because no one can impose their values on us. I am less idealistic than he. When money becomes the only scale of values which counts it's less easy for us to choose our own definition of success. But that, of course, is up to us.

5. Capitalism encourages morality. Without an underlying moral consensus capitalism doesn't work. In parts of Russia today we see a wild economy. Piracy, murder, dishonesty, and a blatant disregard for contracts are widespread. These are held by some to be the inherent features of capitalism which, they say, can only work when its excesses are held in check by a strong and well-enforced legal system. Laws are necessary, but they will only work if people want them to work. Gradually Russia will realize that without a basic understanding of right and wrong in everyday dealings there will be no end to poverty. Capitalism, ironically perhaps, drags morality in its train, rather than the other way round.

6. Capitalism builds community. Businesses don't work, as I shall argue later on, unless they are communities. For many, the workplace, or nowadays, more accurately, the work system, has been their prime community. Indeed, if we lose that sense of community the business becomes a

mere box of individual contracts. The good business encourages reliability and fidelity in personal relationships and turns us into competent human beings, prepared to work for a common cause.

These arguments describe capitalism as it could and should be. Creativity, choice and responsibility, morality and community are the fruits of capitalism. The trouble is they are also its fuel. Without them it degenerates into a jungle where the devil takes the hindmost. We cannot expect capitalism to take care of itself. It is only a tool, and tools can be used and misused. Life, and the purpose of life, is something else again.

Keynes, turning from economics to philosophy in his 1930 essay "Economic Possibilities for Our Grandchildren" foresaw it all.

We are being afflicted with a new disease of which some readers may not yet have heard the name, but of which they will hear a great deal in the years to come—namely *technological unemployment*. This means unemployment due to our discovery of means of economizing the use of labor outrunning the pace at which we can find new uses for labor. . . . This means that the economic problem is not, if we look into the future, the permanent problem of the human race.

Keynes goes on to say that once the economic problem is solved, mankind will be deprived of its traditional purpose and will be faced with the real problem, which economics will have won: how to live wisely, agreeably, and well. He doesn't think that this will be welcomed by all. "There is no country and no people, I think, who can look forward to the age of abundance without dread." But, ultimately, "when the accumulation of wealth is no longer of high social importance, there will be great changes in the code of morals . . . we shall be able to assess the money motive at its true value."

Nothing changes. Capitalism, no matter how successful, will never on its own give a complete answer to the question "why?" We may look for solutions in better management theories, ones that actually take account of the limits of humanity as well as of its potential, or in a new economics which counts the real worth of something, not just its cost. But both these reforms can only be driven, if they ever happen, by a better understanding of what we want from life, both for ourselves and for others. Ultimately, we need a new understanding of life, one that gives money its due, but not more than its due.

Capitalism is too strong for governments. If we want to control it we must do so ourselves. It will take the collective will of many individuals to make the market our servant rather than our master. For that to happen those individuals have to be clear about who they are, why they think that they exist, and what they want from life. Not, unfortunately, as easy to do as to say, but crucial if we want to have control of our own lives and of our society.

Adam Smith believed that virtuous men, or women, on their own, changed nothing, unless the system changed as well. He is, however, the lasting proof that good ideas, at the right time, can change systems, if the virtuous people help. Good ideas are, usually, not new ideas, but old ideas resurrected at the right time. Maybe the time is ripe for the resurrection of some old philosophies of life and society.

Vaclav Havel, playwright, dissident, prisoner, and president of the Czech Republic, spelled out the challenge:

The salvation of this human world lies nowhere else than in the human heart, in the human power to reflect, in human meekness and human responsibility. Without a global resolution in human consciousness nothing will change for the better and the catastrophe towards which this world is headed will be unavoidable.

A Life of Our Own

*Capitalism, efficiency, and markets have their flaws,
but also their uses. They are neither the complete answer to our dilemmas nor the only cause of them. They
provide some of the context of our lives but not the
purpose. For that we need a philosophy not an economic system.*

*In this part of the book I examine the quest for a
purpose in our own lives. I suggest that the purpose
has to be an attempt to leave the world a little better
than we found it. Forced to be free to shape our own
lives, we can, by example and initiative, slowly
change the part of the world around us. That process,
however, starts with us and our own lives. Our duty to*

others is founded on our duty to ourselves. It seems a self-centered and selfish place to start, but selfishness can be "proper" and for the good of others. In any case, we have no choice. More than ever before, we are on our own, left to forge our own destinies.

The Age of Personal Sovereignty

I N 1959 I went to Moscow on my way back to my first job as an oil executive in Malaysia. It was unusual and difficult, at that time, to go to Russia as a tourist. The only flights into Russia were from Copenhagen, and every visitor had to have an escort throughout his or her stay, an Intourist guide, supposedly for your convenience. Mine was an attractive young woman so I wasn't objecting too much. We got on well.

One day she said to me, "Is it true that in your country you have to find your own job and your own place to live?"

"Yes, of course," I replied.

"Oh, how frightening for you," she exclaimed. "I wouldn't like that at all."

"We call it freedom," I said, rather smugly, and thanked my lucky stars that I didn't live in Russia.

It was only later, on the plane leaving Russia en route to my oil company, that I realized that my benevolent employers also told me what job to do and where to live, and would do so for the rest of my working life. In those days they also insisted on the right to approve my choice of wife, and once we were married, they wrote appraisals on her as well as me, arguing that, if we were to represent them in the far corners of the world, they had a right to make sure that the other half of the partnership was up to scratch. They don't do that anymore, I hasten to add, but in the 1960s the practice was not unusual among international firms.

Of course it was true that I had the freedom to make that big initial choice of what work to do and which firm to apply to, but my Russian guide had also had that initial choice. She could have decided to be a space scientist or a teacher, and, had she been good enough, a job would have been found for her. We weren't, perhaps, so different after all.

I left my oil company after ten years, when I refused their offered posting and they said that, sorry, there was nothing else available. Looking back now, I am amazed that I was, initially, both pleased and proud to have handed over my life to that company. Good as the company was, and is, as an employer, it was *my* life and *my* destiny and I wanted to be responsible for both. Not everybody in that company felt the same way, I must add. Many liked being chucked around the world, knowing that they would retire with a generous pension, a nice collection of mementoes of faraway places, and some good stories to tell. It can be cold outside, as I soon discovered.

You didn't have to join an international oil company to have your life arranged for you. Many large organizations aspired to do the same, whether in business, government, or the professions. People generally made one big choice at the start of their careers and hoped that their working life was then settled for the duration. For some it was the mines, for others "the works" or the farm, for others the family firm, the church, teaching, medicine, or the law. If you were a woman, and this was not that long ago, marriage was, usually, the important initial decision. After that, life would be organized for you, like it or not. In America and most Western countries, at that time, there were "finishing schools" for young women of the richer classes which explicitly set out to prepare them for married life, a life which did not envisage careers or paid work outside the home. They learned such things as flower arranging, glove-making, household management, and the arts of conversation—on the assumption that the rest of life would be dictated by their husband-to-be.

THE NEW ERA

The real social revolution of the last thirty years, one we are still living through, is the switch from a life that is largely organized for us, once we have opted into it, to a world in which we are all forced to be in charge of our own destiny. An evolution in social values, pushed by breakthroughs in technology—the contraceptive pill as much as the computer—and a more competitive world in which changes are forced on us whether we like them or not, all conspire to loosen the bonds between institutions and individuals. Whether the institutions be those of work, of marriage, or of community, the contracts now seem to be endlessly renegotiable. For some this is exciting freedom. We can write our own script for our life instead of acting out a part that someone else has written for us. For others it is a horrible insecurity.

It is tempting to deny that this new era of personal sovereignty is happening to any great extent, or, alternatively, to assert that it has always been this way, and that I am exaggerating the stability of the past and the hold of the institutions. It is true that there have always been many exceptions to the general rule of an ordered life. It is also true that the expectations of an ordered life did not always, or even often, work out. Nevertheless, my recollections of my generation, growing up forty years ago, are that we accepted, largely without too much questioning, that our life would not be completely our own to organize, whatever we were going to do. Distasteful though it was, a society structured around class, property, and education was a more predictable place if you were content to accept the place where you found yourself. I am sure that life was even more structured in earlier generations. Long ago, Plato believed that a properly structured society, in which all knew their place, was the basis of a just society, and many have since agreed with him—particularly if they were at, or near, the top of that society.

Today, the divorce statistics and, more interestingly, perhaps, the new varieties of family illustrate how much has changed on the domestic front. It is accepted as a matter of course that women should have the choices that men have always had and, to a large extent, that we can choose who should or should not make up our families. Anna Brooks-Kastel, a fifteen-year-old schoolgirl, spoke for many when she said in a newspaper interview:

> I've got two mums and two dads, lots of brothers and sisters, and none of them are actually whole. They are all half and steps and bits and bobs and I love them. I just call them my brothers and sisters because that's what they feel like. If they're talking about love from your family I suppose you should have as many

parents as physically possible. Everyone you consider family is family. Friends can be family.

Not everyone would want such a flexible family, but more and more people are experiencing some version of it. At work, the labor market facts are also there for all to see, although some prefer not to look at them. Most of our lives are now only loosely linked to institutions. In America, the official statistics suggest that 37 percent of workers are now "outside" the organization, being either part-time or temporary (26 percent), self-employed (6 percent) or unemployed (5 percent). In Britain the percentage "outside" has grown to 51 percent with other European countries flickering between America and Britain. Many people, particularly those in governments, wish that this were not so, because it is tidier and more predictable to have people inside organizations where they can be provided for—and taxed—more conveniently. It is tempting for such people to interpret the statistics rather differently.

The following table, taken from a study prepared for the British government in 1996, illustrates both the situation and the source of the confusion.

TYPE OF EMPLOYMENT	PERCENTAGE OF BRITISH LABOR FORCE		
	1985	1995	2005
Part-Time	21	24	25
Self-Employed	11	13	13.5
Temporary	5	6	8
Permanent	84	82	79

Source: Labor Market Flexibility. Business Strategies, London.

If you add the unemployment figures (8 percent in 1995) to the combined total of part-timers, self-employed, and temporary, you arrive at a figure of 51 percent for 1995. In other words more than half the available workforce does not have a proper full-time job inside an organization. This is the outward and visible sign of the new flexibility, which many believe to be essential if we are to remain agile enough to keep up with the changing world. The defenders of the status quo, however, point to the "permanent" figures, which, they argue, show that the great bulk of the work-force is still in permanent employment, although what "perma-nent" means when applied to part-timers or the self-employed is hard to work out.

It is also true that the average length of a job has hardly changed over the last ten years in Britain or America, remaining constant at around six years. A full-time career is, therefore, a succession of six-year jobs. This, again, is a rather narrow inter-pretation of "permanent," and no one has yet established how many of these six-year jobs now make up a career. What is clear is that many people are opting out of the official workforce ear-lier than they used to, in their early or late fifties, and that those holding those six-year jobs are now only a minority of the work-force.

Whatever the correct numbers, it is clear that the psychologi-cal contract between employers and employees has changed. The smart jargon now talks of guaranteeing "employability" not "employment," which, being interpreted, means don't count on us, count on yourself, but we'll try to help if we can. No longer can anyone expect to be able to hand over their lives to an organization for more than something like six years. After that you are on your own again, either by your initiative or theirs, and can only hope that you are, indeed, as employable as was prom-ised. We are, in effect, all mercenaries now, on hire to the highest bidder, and useful as long as, and only as long as, we can perform.

> In such a world, it is wise and prudent not to make long-term plans or invest in the distant future; not to get tied down too firmly to any particular place, group or cause, even to an image of oneself, because one might find oneself not just un-anchored and drifting but without an anchor altogether; it is prudent to be guided in today's choices not by the wish to *control* the future, but by the reluctance to *mortgage* it. In other words, "to be provident" means now, more often than not, to avoid *commitment*. To be free to move when opportunity knocks. To be free to leave when it stops knocking.

The words are not mine. They come from Zygmunt Bauman, one of the world's most distinguished philosophers, in *Alone Again: Ethics After Certainty*. It is an essay for our times. Bauman is worried by the privatization of society—not the vogue for turning every state activity into a business, although that is part of the argument, but the fact that, increasingly, we now belong to, or are committed to, nothing besides ourselves. Even the family can often turn out to be a relationship of convenience, to be discontinued if it doesn't suit. At work, our loyalty and responsibility are first to ourselves and our future, secondly to our current group or project, and only lastly, and minimally, to the organization.

Without commitment to anyone or anything else, however, there is no sense of responsibility for others, and without responsibility there is no need for morality—anything goes, or at least anything that is legal, if it's what you want. To be a citizen seems to mean nothing much more than being a customer, letting others make decisions which you can then take or leave, or take and then complain about. "I pay my taxes, don't I?" was the response of one chairman when asked what responsibility he felt for the thousands whom he had just declared redundant. Taxes, in fact, are now seen as the way we discharge our responsibilities to the rest of the community, and, understandably, we wish to pay as few of those as possible and to leave it to others to decide how to spend them while we get on with our own lives.

It may all be a rational response to a chaotic world, one where the future is there to be invented, not predicted, and certainly not to be controlled; but it makes for a lonely world, one in which the neighborhood is a jungle, the stranger a beast to hide from, and our home a privatized prison. Bauman quotes Max Frisch: "We can now do what we want, and the only question is what do we want? At the end of our progress we stand where Adam and Eve once stood; and all we are faced with now is the moral question."

There lies the rub. I take a more positive view of what William Rees-Mogg has called individual sovereignty. As I see it, we have been put back in charge of our lives. We can do with them what we like. Given that know-how or know-what, plus energy and initiative, are the new sources of wealth, anyone can in theory earn a living. The question then is "what sort of living does one want?" The words "in theory" are, of course, important. There are huge structural impediments to individual wealth creation. Many don't have the know-how, or the initiative or the will. Somehow they must be helped to acquire these things, if the idea of personal sovereignty is not going to seem like some sort of obscene joke perpetrated on a permanent underclass.

That is our most urgent priority in the new century. But it won't be tackled unless we deal with the more fundamental question of "what do we want" both for ourselves and, by extension, for others, because Immanuel Kant was right: you can't, in all equity, propose one set of rules for yourself, and something else for everyone else. Without some commonly accepted agreement on the purpose of life, and on the proper balance between what we can expect and what is expected from us, society becomes a battleground, where the devil takes the hindmost. Max Frisch spoke the truth; it *is* a moral question.

As things stand we seem to be saying that life is essentially about economics, that money is the measure of most things, and that the market is its sorting mechanism. My hunch is that most of us don't believe any of this, and that it won't work, for reasons given earlier, but we are trapped in our own rhetoric and have, as yet, nothing else to offer, not even a different way to talk about it. There is, I believe, a hunger for something else which might be more enduring and more worthwhile.

CORPORATE SOVEREIGNTY

The same sorts of argument apply to corporations. The rhetoric says that businesses are accountable to their owners and are their property and their instruments. In both America and Britain, however, the law has always regarded companies as individuals, who can be sued and held responsible, not as inanimate pieces of property, whose owners are the ones to be held responsible. I think that the law has it right. A company is a person. The concept of ownership is, I suggest, deeply flawed in this new era. For one thing, what is it that the owners own? The value of most businesses these days lies in their invisible assets, their accumulated skills and experience, their brands, research, and managerial ability. It is hard to see how anyone can "own" such things, which are largely tied up with particular human beings, each of whom is free to walk away at any time.

Secondly, most of the owners of any public corporation have, in fact, put no money into the business. The stock market is a secondary market in which shares change hands without any of the money going anywhere near the business. "Shareholders" is an accurate description of the notional owners, but they should, more truthfully, be regarded as investors rather than owners. As investors, they need to be kept happy, not least to keep the share price high, although I would argue that the Anglo-American tradition of high dividends prices happiness too high. Large dividends paid out to shareholders can bleed the company of the money it needs for the future, since there are few opportunities for happy investors to put their dividends back into the same business, as true owners might want to do. Some organizations are now using their profits to buy back their own shares, leading some commentators to wonder what happens when a corporation owns 100 percent of its stock, and is then legally responsible only to itself.

For all practical purposes, however, organizations are already responsible only to themselves. As long as they keep their investors happy, businesses are, by and large, free to do what they like. If you, as an investor, don't like what they do, you can always leave. If your investment is so large that you can't conveniently leave, you can, in the last resort, get rid of the top people and put in some replacements who will, you hope, do something better. That is not necessarily an act of ownership, but the last resort of worried investors.

In practical terms, therefore, businesses are responsible only to themselves, for what they do and how they do it. In the real world, a well-managed business pays very close attention to its various constituencies, or stakeholders, because it wants to keep not only its investors happy but, even more so, its customers, its workforce, and its suppliers, and, necessarily, the surrounding community, because it is hard to grow any business in a desert or a slum. Keeping all these constituencies happy does not necessarily mean that it is accountable to them for anything else. Provided they all profit in some way from it, the business can decide for itself what it stands for and what its goals are. Well-run businesses make a lot of money because they do the right things right, but it doesn't stop there. The real question is, what is the money, the profit, going to be used for, and in what manner will it be used? For that we have to trust the people who manage the business, the new professionals.

This is the age of the professionals, in business as in everything else. Strangely, there are few true capitalists now, in this the flowering of the capitalist age, only the agents of the savers— agents who are professionals themselves: the pension funds, insurance groups, and mutual funds, investing on the behalf of the ordinary person. They do not consider themselves to be owners, only investors. Our wealth, therefore, is increasingly in the hands of those professionals who either manage or work with the corporations. They are supposedly in charge of the sovereign corporations and increasingly it is in them that we have to place our trust.

This is particularly true of the transnational corporations, who are more accurately called supranationals, because they float above rather than across the nation-states, owing allegiance to none—or, as they would see it, to every separate state in which they operate. These giant corporations are, in theory, accountable to their shareholders, but the latter, I have argued, are interested only in their dividend stream and not otherwise in how the corporations create their wealth, in faraway places of which they often know nothing.

At the last count, seventy of these giants had revenues bigger than the GNP of Cuba. Like Cuba, they are effectively centrally planned economies, with no serious hints of democracy. Cargill—a family-owned U.S. corporation—has a greater sales turnover in coffee alone than the GNP of any of the African countries from which it buys its coffee beans. Cargill also accounts for over 60 percent of the world trade in cereals. In most countries such a market share would automatically trigger a monopoly inquiry, but Cargill effectively belongs to no country. It is accountable only to itself. I have no reason to believe that Cargill exploits its position. The point is that whether it does or not entirely depends on the values and priorities of the family who own it.

These semi-states are powerful forces in the world, for good or ill. They transfer technology and know-how across borders. They move money more quickly and in greater quantities than any democratic government can. They can make and unmake alliances, take decisions and start things happening with an ease and a speed that any ordinary state must envy. And they can do almost all of this without consulting anybody beyond those directly concerned. Unlike other states, they are not part of the United Nations, or subject to its resolutions. They are answerable to no one save their own investors.

One day, the nation-states may try to have some say in the governance of these free-roving alternative states. Until then, we really have to rely on the companies' own sense of their proper purpose, which starts with the essential need to be profitable but must then answer the "what for?" question. The late David Packard, co-founder and inspiration of Hewlett Packard, one of the world's most respected international businesses, put it this way, shortly before he died:

Why are we here? I think many people assume, wrongly, that a company exists solely to make money. Money is an important part of a company's existence, if the company is any good. But a result is not a cause. We have to go deeper and find the real reason for our being. As we investigate this, we inevitably come to the conclusion that a group of people get together and exist as an institution that we call a company, so that they are able to accomplish something collectively that they could not accomplish separately—they make a contribution to society, a phrase which sounds trite but is fundamental.

Great companies aren't shy about saying, publicly, why they exist. James Collins and Jerry Porras collected a few examples in their research on successful long-lasting companies:

> MARY KAY COSMETICS: To give unlimited opportunity to women.
> MERCK: To preserve and improve human life.
> SONY: To experience the joy of advancing and applying technology for the benefit of the public.
> WAL-MART: To give ordinary folk the chance to buy the same things as rich people.
> WALT DISNEY: To make people happy.

Assuming that they mean what they say, you can understand why people might want to work for these companies, even if it is only for six years. Such companies have a personality and what some have called a soul. You can almost smell it, when it is there. I once asked my students to walk into an office or a plant and, without speaking to anyone, to make a guess at what kind of environment it would be to work in, and what kind of attitudes and values the management would hold. They were amazed at how accurate their guesses turned out to be when we later visited the same places more formally and conducted surveys of the staff.

I maintain that companies are no different from individuals, or vice versa. Both are responsible for their own destinies, and for their own behavior. Both need to work out their underlying purpose, which is what gives them their uniqueness. They cannot pass that buck, and there are relatively few constraints on what they choose to do, provided that it is within the law. That is both the opportunity and the risk. For some, however, the thought that we are in charge of our own destiny is either bad science or bad religion. If they are right, then this book is subversive. What we believe about these things matters hugely.

THE GERANIUM THEORY

I was sitting on a terrace in Italy talking these matters over with a friend. "I don't see why you bother about these philosophical pedantries," he said. "That geranium over there doesn't, and it seems to be thriving."

"But I'm not a geranium," I replied indignantly.

"What makes you think you are any different? You may look different, and have more faculties, and live longer, but, basically, that's all we are, sophisticated geraniums. So lie back and enjoy it. Do what your instincts tell you. May I fill your glass?"

"But if you were a geranium, wouldn't you want to be a better geranium?" I asked.

"Only if my strain of geranium was a self-improving sort, in which case I would still be following my geranium instincts, but it wouldn't make me a morally better geranium, just, maybe, the sort of geranium that people would want to propagate."

I realized that I was heading into the territory of Edward Wilson, the sociobiologist, and of Richard Dawkins. Dawkins writes seductively about the selfish gene in books like *The Blind Watchmaker* and *River out of Eden*, arguing in a neo-Darwinian fashion that we are, in every way, the product of our inherited genes, that even our religious impulses, if we have any, are inherited tendencies. It was an argument that I could not win, because, whatever I said, my friend would come back and say, "But, of course, you are that sort of geranium and so you are programmed that way."

It's a tempting idea, this sort of genetic determinism, because it suggests that feelings of responsibility for anything are merely inherited characteristics. Neuroscience, an academic discipline which deals with some of these issues, is one of the fastest growing areas of study in the United States. The Society for Neuroscience, formed in 1970 with 1,100 members, now has 26,000. Neuroscientists have been heard to say that, given powerful enough computers, it should eventually be possible to predict the course of any human's life moment by moment, including that person's reaction to this news.

The sudden switch from nurture, in the form of social conditioning, to nature, in the form of genetics and brain physiology, may yet turn out to be one of the major intellectual events of this end of the century. To listen to the new nature enthusiasts, it matters not how you were brought up, or what school you went to. Forget Freud. Your type of geranium was all predetermined as soon as you were conceived. Social policy is mere wishful thinking, bound to be unavailing against the forces of nature. If, therefore, you don't happen to have any of those feelings of responsibility that are so important to others, don't worry. Relax, just be what you feel you are. You have no other choice.

That's why determinism is dangerous. Even if it is true, we can't afford to believe it. It can be interpreted, probably misinterpreted, as a license for the crudest form of selfishness, a recipe for an amoral society at best, and an immoral one at worst.

Businesses sometimes relish this sort of thinking. They like to see themselves as economic entities in the grip of forces greater than themselves. They are what they have to be in order to survive in the Darwinian world of economics. Such a philosophy allows them to exploit their customers or their suppliers or even their employees as long as they can get away with it. Geraniums have short but often sunny lives. So it is with many get-rich-quick businesses who think that the idea of a contribution to society is just a lot of woolly wish-wash, about as relevant, to them, as grace before meals.

Others would put the argument more positively. If you pursue the bottom line, subjecting yourself to the law of the market-place, everything else—the way you treat employees, suppliers and, most importantly, customers—will fall into place. We are the pawns of the marketplace, driven by its imperatives. We need have no will of our own other than to succeed on its terms. The market will keep us honest.

This whole issue is critically important. There is no point in worrying about what we want out of life and for life, if we really have no choice. Responsibility, then, to oneself or anyone else, is a non-concept and the whole of this book is a waste of paper. Stop reading at once if that is your view. There can be no absolute proof of either philosophy. It is what we ourselves choose to believe that influences our lives. Beliefs surface when the facts run out, or when the facts are not yet proven.

The truth probably is that our genes give us certain predispositions—to be athletic, or mathematical, or linguistically skilled, or none of these, like me—on top of which we pile the impact of our early environment. Each of us reaches adulthood with a different starter package. But that isn't the end of the story, only the beginning. What we do with it is still up to us. You don't have to put your faith in a creator God who makes us different from the animals. You can believe, as I do, that humans are more than animated geraniums, that we have evolved into beings with a capacity for self-awareness which allows us to influence our own behavior if we so decide. Jean-Jacques Rousseau was more dogmatic: "There is one further distinguishing characteristic of man which is very specific indeed and about which there can be no dispute, and that is the faculty of self-improvement."

It is this self-awareness that enables us to work out a distinction between right and wrong, without any necessity to believe that the same sense of right and wrong was inborn in all of us. It is this self-awareness that allows us to develop the idea of progress, an idea which scientists agree is not naturally there in the process of evolution. It is this self-awareness, finally, that carries with it a concept of responsibility that goes beyond any genetic disposition to protect one's own. For if biology is as genetically competitive and relentlessly opportunistic as we have been led to believe, and if there is no sense of progress in that process, no sense of purpose, if it's all just a biological free-for-all, then purpose is something which we humans can and must impose on science.

However, the reason that I reject the idea of a dominant determinism is that I would find life totally meaningless unless I believed that I had the capacity to influence it. Whether that feeling is genetically produced in me, or whether it comes about from my self-awareness working overtime, is irrelevant. Even Richard Dawkins says that he drew attention to the selfish gene not to justify it, but to encourage us "to rebel against the tyranny of the selfish replicators." I believe that I can make a dent in the world around me, for good or ill, and that is what, in the end, makes life interesting. My hope is that most people feel the same, deep down.

THE RELIGIOUS OPTION

Many people would regard my aspirations as arrogant humanism. We are, they argue, the instruments of God's purpose, or, in a more atheistic and communist language, the agents of society. We should put our trust in Him, or maybe Her, and be guided by the teaching and tradition of the particular religion to which we adhere. It is not up to us to decide how or when to try to improve on God's creation. I have known several devout men and women who genuinely feel that they are led by God to do what they do, and what they do is obviously of great help and comfort to others. I have little doubt that they are in touch with some inner voice or drive which conditions their behavior. It would not be going too far to describe them as holy or saintly.

I have, however, known others for whom the religious option is a way of escaping responsibility. "I asked God to find me a job," said one young man. "He didn't, so I assume that He wants me to remain unemployed." For others a slavish interpretation of the rules of their religion is what life is about. Do the right thing always and everything will come out all right. Theirs is not to reason why, to argue with the pope or the archbishop, or to question the views of the hierarchy. This unquestioning obedience is what has given organized religions their power, both for good and, too often, for evil, down the ages.

The increasing interest in revivalist and charismatic religions may be one response to the increasing uncertainty of the modern world. It is a search for another sort of certainty, one unconnected with the material universe. Some would even argue that the only proper concern of religion is this other universe, an argument which becomes an invitation to detach oneself from things and money and jobs. Those in charge of this more mundane world are often only too happy to encourage this otherworldly stance, wanting no transcendent values to intrude into their pragmatic concerns.

My understanding of religion is different. Religion offers a second-order certainty, an assurance that there is a purpose to our lives. It does not, and should not, offer any first-order certainty, any prescription of what that purpose should be. That remains our individual responsibility. The freedom to choose is our splendid prerogative, God-given or not, along with the freedom to choose wrongly. Choice and the chance of sin go together. You can't have one without the other. To be sure, there have always been great exemplars and great teachers in all the religions, and there is much that can be learned from them. The Bible is as good a philosophical textbook as you will find anywhere. The rule books of the religions, however, have been as much about social order as about the right purpose of our lives. They are not to be despised for that but they are what they are— rule books, not invitations to stop thinking.

It is because religions can stop one thinking for oneself that they can mislead, turning people into zealots, even into terrorists on occasion. In that sense they are akin to the geranium view of life. Our life, they suggest, is not our responsibility. Our duty is but to go where we are bidden, or where we think we are bidden. That is religion as false certainty, as escapism not engagement. It is, for that reason, misleading and dangerous.

Properly understood, the religious approach offers us ways to get in touch with our true selves, in particular with the good that lies in each of us. I have been in places which resonate with holiness—once, a lonely chapel attached to a farmhouse in Tuscany where monks had prayed for generations but had left not a visible mark or ornament behind, just the trace of their presence and their prayers. You cannot be in such places without examining your conscience and reflecting on your life. To be quiet and still, somewhere, each day, as a discipline, purges the mind. Call it prayer or meditation if you wish. Beauty in all its forms, great music, fine buildings, these all uplift the soul, and can't be bad. Religious rituals reinvigorate you, at their best. They pull you in, allow you to cleanse yourself of the things you are ashamed of, lift you up and push you out into the world again, Turkish baths for the soul.

Religion like this is a great aid to self-responsibility. It might even be essential. But it is religion without the creeds and without the hierarchies. It is the religion of doubt and uncertainty, offering one the strength to persevere, to find one's own way in a world that is, inevitably, very different from any world that was known to those who went before.

I find it necessary to reject the false certainties of both religion and science in order to discharge what I feel to be the responsibility for my own destiny. I believe this to be a responsibility which falls on every one of us. We cannot duck out of it.

Proper Selfishness

I SPENT THE early part of my life trying hard to be someone
else. At school I wanted to be a great athlete, at university an
admired socialite, afterwards a businessman and, later, the head
of a great institution. It did not take me long to discover that I
was not destined to be successful in any of these guises, but that
did not prevent me from trying, and being perpetually disappointed with myself. The problem was that in trying to be someone else I neglected to concentrate on the person I could be.
That idea was too frightening to contemplate at the time. I was
happier going along with the conventions of the time, measuring
success in terms of money and position, climbing ladders which
others placed in my way, collecting things and contacts rather
than giving expression to my own beliefs and personality.

I was, in retrospect, hiding from myself, a slave to the system
rather than its master. We can't, however, discover ourselves by
introspection. We have to jump in before we learn to swim. That

is hardly a new discovery. The idea that true individuality is necessarily social is one of the oldest propositions in philosophy. We find ourselves through what we do and through the long struggle of living with and for others. "I do therefore I am" is more real than "I think therefore I am."

It was Pascal who said that all the ills in the world come about because a man cannot sit in a room alone. But also all the good things come about, surely, because most of the delights of life come from our association with other people. To be "shut up in the solitude of his own heart"—what de Tocqueville saw as the danger of extreme individualism in America—is not something to be desired. As Peter Singer, the Australian philosopher, puts it, to be completely self-absorbed and self-sufficient is equivalent to spending your life writing your autobiography—there is nothing to write about, except writing the autobiography. To be ourselves we need other people.

What I term a "proper selfishness" builds on this fact that we are inevitably intertwined with others—even if sometimes we wish that we weren't—but accepts that it's proper to be concerned with ourselves and a search for who we really are. That search should lead us to realize that self-respect, in the end, only comes from responsibility, responsibility for other people and other things. Proper selfishness is not escapism. Paradoxically, as I have suggested, we only really find ourselves when we lose ourselves in something beyond ourselves, be it our love for someone, our pursuit of a cause or a vocation, or our commitment to a group or an institution. Forced to be selfish by the changes in the world around us, we have the choice to make it proper. If more of us so choose, we can make the systems work for us rather than the other way round.

In the third part of this book I shall explore some ways in which, by applying this philosophy to the institutions of society, we could make some practical changes and improvements to our world. But the philosophy has to start with us. What that means in practice is the subject of these next chapters.

THE HUNGRY SELF

"Get a life" is not just a catchy phrase. It is, says Timothy Gorringe, the theologian, the only ethical imperative. The British journalist Michael Bywater has described his feelings after a friend had a liver transplant operation. He wondered, he said, what it felt like to have someone else's part inside of you. What sort of life had to end before his friend could start to live again? Was the donor a man? A woman? How old? What did they do? Did they like croissants for breakfast, enjoy making love, see their life as a failure, hope for the future, wish for the end? Did they polish the car on the day it killed them in the accident? Had they ever written a book, planted a tree, wept over a Brahms symphony, had a religious vision, eaten snails, held a newborn baby, licked their lover all over, stolen money, owned a kangaroo-hide stock-whip, had their pocket picked, sung in public, declared all the love they had to declare? And what duty, he asked, do we owe them, to carry on the imagined life they may have lived?

All we know, Bywater concludes, is that, whatever else they did, they saved a life. So perhaps his friend's duty is therefore to live that life. Perhaps that's true for all of us. You don't have to have a transplant for that to make sense.

If we are human we must choose life, but that begs the question nicely—what is this thing called life? Life surely is the chance to make the best of ourselves. We owe it to everybody to give them that chance, even if they make a mess of it. We can detect in each of us a tendency towards good and the opposite tendency towards evil. We could argue whether these tendencies come from God or from our genes, but perhaps, if you believe that God is the mastermind behind the universe, it comes to the same thing. The proper, or decent, self is one where the good is revealed and the evil restrained. Most of us are hungry for a self of which we can be proud. More and more people, especially the young, in the affluent societies of the West, share this hunger. Paul Ray, an American sociologist, calls these hungry people Transmoderns and believes that they account for a quarter of all Americans. Walk into any American bookstore and marvel at the number of books whose titles include the word "soul," even in the business section.

Proper selfishness starts by reinterpreting self-interest, insisting that it is more than economics. The decade of the eighties, when for a time "greed was good" as Ivan Boesky famously put it, made money the measure of success and defined self-interest as looking after your own financial future. Margaret Thatcher, in her heyday, talked of self-responsibility, not selfishness. But, because she failed to define what the self could or should be, she was understood to mean self-interest, and short-term monetary interest at that, financial selfishness. That was unfortunate, because self-interest cannot be seen simply in monetary terms, even by the most materially minded. It is important to correct the definition, because if our self is more than an economic item, then growth based on self-interest has to mean much more than economic growth. Many of those who found riches in the eighties were still hungry for something more at the end of the decade, for money may be necessary but can never be sufficient to satisfy all our hopes for ourselves.

One tradition, the Christian one, has it that life is not about the satisfaction of needs, although that is inevitably part of it, but the chance to test oneself against all the challenges and so to prove oneself. Money will form a part of this type of self-interest, but only a part.

My own children, like many of the children of the middle-classes in the West, have never known real poverty or the threat of death in war. I, on the other hand, grew up in a time when the threat of war was real, when the memories of starvation were still alive in Europe, only slowly recovering from the last war. It was quite possible that I would die in battle as many of the parents and grandparents of my generation had done. Life was, I knew, going to be a struggle for survival and would possibly be quite short. The priorities were clear, practical, and dominated by economics.

It is different now. "Our young are not hungry enough" the elders of Japan complain, "they don't want to work as we did." They are wrong; the young *are* hungry, but for different things, because, for most of them, poverty and war are taken care of, they hope. Success, then, becomes the spur to our actions, but success, unfortunately, is more difficult to get a handle on than survival. We can buy the definition of that success from those around us or we can, more usefully, find our own definition. The search for that personal definition of success is what drives so many of us today. The more one thinks about it, however, the more it becomes clear that it is really a search for oneself.

THE WHITE STONE

The journey towards self-knowledge is a long and tough one. It needs a jolt to start it, the sort of jolt that comes from a brush with death, divorce, or redundancy. Luke was lucky in a way—he had such a jolt early in his life.

Luke is a young man of West Indian parents. Last year he was down and out and living in London. He had no job, no home, no money, and no hope. There seemed to him to be little point in living. The market economy and the freedom that capitalism offers meant nothing to him. He was outside all of that. By the time I met him, however, there was no trace of that defeatism and depression. He was enrolled in college now, he told me. He was upbeat, charming, interesting in his views—we met at a conference on the future of work—and interested in ours. "What happened?" I asked.

"Well, when things were at their worst, I called my dad and told him how I felt. All he said was, 'Think about this; when you get to heaven you will meet the man you might have been,' then he put the phone down. That was all I needed. I went away, thought about it, and applied to college."

You don't have to believe in a literal heaven to get the point. I keep a small white stone on my desk to remind me of the same point. It refers to a mysterious verse in the Book of Revelations in the Bible, a verse which goes like this: "To the one who prevails, the Spirit says, I will give a white stone . . . on which is written a name, which shall be known only to the one who receives it."

I am no biblical scholar, but I know what I think it means. It means that if I "prevail," I will, eventually, find out who I truly ought to be, the other hidden self. Life is a search for the white stone. It will be a different one for each of us. Of course, it depends on what is meant by "prevail." It means, I suspect, passing life's little tests, until you are free to be fully yourself, which is when you get your white stone.

James Hillman, one of the most respected of America's philosophers of "soul," talks of there being an "acorn" in each of us which contains the seed of our destiny. The Greeks spoke of our *daemon* and the Romans of each person's *genius*. Jesus said the kingdom of God is within us. Today we use words like "spirit," "soul," and "heart." These ideas suggest that our soul is what drives us, if we can only get in touch with it. I favor the symbolism of the white stone because it suggests that we have to take the initiative. To lie back and hope that our soul will lead us to nirvana is not an option.

We have today the opportunity, which is also the challenge, to shape ourselves, even to reinvent ourselves. Our lives are not completely foreordained, either by science or by our souls. We can make of our lives a masterpiece if we so wish. It is an opportunity that ought to be available to all humans. It could be. It is the fortunate combination of liberal democracy and free market capitalism that gives us this opportunity, as long as we make these two our servants, not our masters.

If we knew what was on the white stone to start with, what it meant to be fully yourself, it would all be easy. Since we don't know what it is until we have it, we can only proceed by constant exploration. It is always a long search. Many give up or never start. If it be true, as some hypothesize, that we only discover 25 percent of our potential talents by the time we die—a hypothesis that must remain a conjecture because who would ever know the truth—then the sooner we start experimenting with ourselves the better. I like the idea of a self which can lift itself to unknown heights, a self which exercises self-discipline, postpones gratification, and stops short of aggression in order to discover the very peaks of life. The thought that this might all be preordained by our genes or by our *daemon* is, to me, depressing. It removes any point from life.

"Know Yourself," the ancient Greek admonition, should, logically, be the first step on the way to the white stone. It often, however, turns out to be the end of the quest, not the beginning, because we are growing and changing all the time. It's a wise man that knows his own father, the cynic said, but it's an even wiser one that knows himself before the closing of his days. "To thine own self be true" was Polonius' advice to Laertes, an uncomfortable charge to lay on a young man, who probably had not the slightest idea of who he was at that age and who would have done better to heed the advice of the old Roman, Paracelsus, who advised that if we can't be who we are we should at least not be who we are not—advice I failed to hear myself.

This start on the road to the white stone is not, therefore, an invitation to endless navel-gazing, but a warning not to wear clothes that don't fit you. Stop pretending, in other words, or you waste your life. "Where I am folded in upon myself," said the poet Rilke, "there am I a lie." Look outside first, to find yourself, and do not expect to find the full truth until you have exhausted most of the possibilities, until you are near the end. Death is welcomed by many, because it is the end of searching. Arthur Miller, the playwright, put it like this:

> I see it [life] as an endless, truly endless struggle. There's no time when we're going to arrive at a plateau where the whole thing gets sorted. It's a struggle in the way every plant has to find its own way to stand up straight. A lot of the time it's a failure. And yet it's not a failure if some enlightenment comes out of it.

THE PUZZLE OF IDENTITY

We cannot wait for the approach of death to start the search, however; so how do we go about defining ourselves to start with? Work has always been a major strand in people's self-description, and, therefore, a major component of their identity. Some years ago, my son, then seven, was given a class assignment to write a description of what their fathers did. While disapproving of the assignment on the grounds that it might be discriminatory, I was nevertheless intrigued to know what my son had written. My job at the time, a professor at a business school, was not, I felt, part of his conscious world.

"I said you were a painter," he said.

"Oh," I replied, rather startled by his imagination, because I had never put brush to canvas, but flattered all the same, "what do I paint?"

"Walls," he said, as indeed I had been doing that weekend.

Deflated by his image of me as a painter/decorator, I spent a little time wondering whether it mattered, in his young life, what he thought I did at work. I decided that it didn't. It shouldn't matter to me either.

I was, however, taken aback by the headmaster's reaction when I told him that we were moving, because I had accepted a post as the head of an academic institution in another town. He looked at me, puzzled: "But, how interesting [meaning, how strange]. I thought that you were a decorator."

Was that why, I asked myself, we had received such scant attention from him in the past two years?

Our work role defines us, but only partially. To a degree we are as we are seen by those to whom we are connected—our family, tribe, and friends and colleagues. When I meet my relatives, or my long-standing friends, I am conscious that I am not really interested in their work or career unless it is causing them personal problems. In fact, if they are successful I almost resent it, because it means that they have less time for me. The same is true in reverse—they don't want to hear about books published or lectures delivered. I know and cherish a more personal side of them. My identity, and theirs, is rooted in mutual affection and a shared history. They see a different "me" to the one that others see.

However much we may deny it, the way other people see us does influence the way we see ourselves. Proper selfishness requires that we take our identity into our own care, provided that we give it a reality check with those who know us. We define, for ourselves, who we are and what we stand for. Some people do this with a devil-may-care arrogance, which often conceals a deeper sense of doubt. Others, like myself, are too ready to accept the characterization that others give us—another sign of doubt.

We are all different people in different situations. In one series of portraits my photographer wife shot David, a general, first in his uniform, then in civilian clothes with his wife, and finally in casual garb with his children in the garden. Three very different images of the same person. It is tempting to ask which is the real David. The answer has to be that they are all real at that time, but which one, or which blend, will emerge at the end, imprinted on the white stone, must be for him to find out. It is when the images are too different that life gets confusing. Most of us find that the images come together as we get older, until we become one person, not several.

The moment will arrive when you are comfortable with who you are, and what you are—bald or old or fat or poor, successful or struggling—when you don't feel the need to apologize for anything or to deny anything. To be comfortable in your own skin is the beginning of strength. Derek Walcott, the Nobel Prize–winning poet from the Caribbean, sums up what it feels like when you reach that goal: you will love again the stranger who was yourself.

The time will come
when, with elation,
you will greet yourself arriving
at your own door, in your own mirror,
and each will smile at the other's welcome,

and say, sit here. Eat.
You will love again the stranger who was yourself.
Give wine. Give bread. Give back your heart
to itself, to the stranger who has loved you

all your life, whom you ignored
for another, who knows you by heart.
Take down the love letters from the bookshelf,
the photographs, the desperate notes,
peel your own image from the mirror.
Sit. Feast on your life.

For a long time I sheltered behind my formal title of professor. It was something of which I was greatly proud when I first gained it at the age of thirty-nine, although I remember that my mother's only comment at the time was the hope that this might mean that I would have more time for her grandchildren. By the time I was sixty I was a very part-time professor. My wife urged me to give it up and "grow up," but I feared that I would be in some way naked without a title of some sort to describe me. At conferences they expected both a title and an affiliation to some organization, I told her. When eventually I resigned my professorship and emerged as just "Charles Handy" it was, to my surprise, a great relief.

Women do not seem to have the same hang-up about work titles. Until recently, they had, however, to contend with another tradition, particularly in the Anglo-Saxon countries, under which they were expected to assume their husband's name on marriage, and with it, part of his identity. An important boost to proper selfishness for women came when the assumption of his name became a matter of choice. Out from the shadow of the man, women now have the same problems as men, in shaking off the expectations and stereotypes of society and discovering who they really are. At least, today, they are freer than they were to choose.

Some choose not to choose a life. Victoria Wood, the British comedienne, describes her own life thus:

Born in the North,
Told a few jokes,
Spoiled two bras in the tumble dryer,
Died.

The irony hits a chord, and people laugh, too often recognizing themselves, and a life unexplored. Rachel Lindsey's poem expresses the sadness of that:

It is the world's one crime that its babes grow dull.
Not that they sow, but that they seldom reap.
Not that they serve, but that they have no God to serve.
The tragedy is not death. The tragedy is to die
With commitments undefined, with convictions undeclared
    and with service unfulfilled.

To experiment with one's life is not going to be everyone's choice. It is too risky. That is sad, because we are then condemned to live in the boxes that we make for ourselves, or let others make for us. I first saw Ibsen's great play *The Doll's House* fifteen years ago. The play is about a marriage, a transparently happy one with a successful husband and an attractive, adored, and adoring wife, busying herself, when the play opens, with the gifts and arrangements for Christmas with their three children. In the final denouement, however, that happiness turns out to have been shallow pretense. Nora, the wife, suddenly realizes that she has always been only her husband's doll, a pretty plaything without any identity of her own. It was a role she was happy to accept until she realized what was happening to her. "Yes," she agrees, "I have a duty to my husband and my children, but my first duty is to myself." She departs to make a new life for herself. It would be an interesting exercise to write the sequel.

Great theater shines a mirror on life. I saw some of myself reflected in that mirror. I, too, had a happy marriage but it was very centered on myself. It was time, I belatedly realized, that my wife had more opportunity to explore her own white stone and to escape from the box that we had both unwittingly created for her. She earned a degree in photography, receiving her results on the exact same day that our son heard his. She has since developed her own individual approach to portrait photography, one which happens to be pertinent to the puzzle of identity.

In one series of portraits she gave the person being photographed a range of prints to choose from. That person chose quite different ones for her mother, her partner, her children, and herself. Unconsciously she was revealing the different faces of herself—her different boxes. In another instance Elizabeth did it the other way round, asking the different members of the family to choose the image of their relation that they liked best. None of them chose the same, because each had a different image of who she was. For this woman, the exposure of her different faces became the start of a journey in search of herself.

In the large Japanese organizations they don't promote the best and the brightest of their young people as quickly as we do in the West. Instead they rotate them through a variety of jobs on the same level. I christened it their horizontal fast track. They want these talented people to have the chance to experience a range of options and a variety of superiors so that they will not necessarily be defined by their education as an engineer or a lawyer when their real skills lie elsewhere. It is an opportunity to escape from the boxes into which they have slipped, perhaps without a great deal of thought. In these days of independence, young would-be managers use the MBA degree partly as a qualification but also as a chance to redefine themselves, to escape from the box of their past.

Consider, however, the plight of the unemployed man whom I met as one of a series of people I was interviewing for a radio program. He had no job, no family, and, as far as I could ascertain, no friends and no permanent home. He had a name and a very positive personality, but no reference points in society. He was completely free to compose his own identity but had nothing and no one to bounce it up against, no data to work on, no portraits to give, and no one to give them to. As far as he knew, his view of himself might be a complete fantasy. There was no sense of proper selfishness there, no basis for any further exploration of life. His only box was one labeled "unemployed," which is a difficult one to escape from. Perhaps the first step is to relabel that box—as self-employed, maybe.

For me, his experience contained an important clue. Identity requires responsibility, because without responsibility there is no self-respect. You do not know whether you could handle anything, deliver any result, or take care of anyone else. You don't know if your sense of "you" works, because there is no reality check. Work, of some sort, therefore becomes almost essential. It doesn't have to be formal work in a job. A friend describes how the birth of her baby daughter with severe cerebral palsy gave her real responsibility for the first time in her life, a feeling of true worth and the experience of unconditional love. The practical problems, for she is a single mother, are immense, but she now knows who she is and what her life is for. Exhausted though she is, for most of the time, she has never looked happier.

If personal responsibility is the key to identity and self-respect there are important educational and policy issues which follow. They will be discussed in the third part of the book.

THE THREE STEPS

No one finds the white stone all at once, or early. There is, it seems, a necessary sequence which we have to experience.

Francis Kinsman, in a book too little noticed at the time, called *Millennium, Towards Tomorrow's Society,* written at the end of the materialistic eighties, used three psychological types developed by the Stanford Research Institute to describe the world as he saw it. The three types are:

Sustenance Driven
Outer Directed
Inner Directed

Ugly words for important truths. So ugly, in fact, that at first I misunderstood them. *Outer directed* I assumed meant concerned *for* other people. In fact, as we shall see, it means being concerned *with what other people do or think,* their values and their preoccupations. *Inner directed* turns out to be what Jung would call individuation and what I think of as proper selfishness, an ability to work out your own values and purposes. Technical terms are good, however, once you understand them, because they are unemotive. For my own ease of understanding and everyday usage I have relabelled the Stanford categories as survival, achievement, and self-expression, but these terms don't have the same precision as Stanford's. Here are the Stanford definitions:

✳ SUSTENANCE DRIVEN

The prime objective of sustenance-driven people is security, both financial and social. Although some of them are poor and/or unemployed, others are comfortably off but want to cling to what they have. Such people are clannish, set in their ways, and resistant to change. They are, says Kinsman, "the left-over philosophical products of the agricultural era—the top, middle and bottom of the feudal heap."

✳ OUTER DIRECTED

Outer-directed people are high achievers. They are searching for esteem and status, as the outward symbols of their success in life. They want, therefore, to have the best, or at least the right, things in life. They are usually intelligent, well educated, and ambitious. They are materialistic, except in those circles where it is smart not to be materialistic. They are the driving force behind economically successful societies.

✳ INNER DIRECTED

The driving force of these people is to give expression to their talents and beliefs. This does not imply that they are withdrawn or aloof or, even, unambitious, but they tend to be less materialistic than the other two groups, more concerned with ethics and the way society is run. Their values are based on personal growth, self-fulfillment, sensibility, and the quality of their and other people's lives. The others call them "wimps," says Kinsman, yet some others find them dangerous. "How can we identify these people—and stamp them out?" asked one authoritarian manager.

Kinsman uses these categories to draw pictures of society as it might develop in the new millennium. Taking data from international surveys, he sees a gradual shift from sustenance to outer directed and from outer to inner directed, although countries differ markedly. In 1989 inner-directed individuals accounted for 36 percent of the British population and 42 percent of the Dutch. The Germans, however, had more outer directeds than any other country, while Italy and France, still with strong agrarian cultures in some areas, were strikingly sustenance driven. America varied by region, as one might expect, California and New England having double the percentage of inner-directed people as the national average, up alongside the British, but with the percentage falling to single figures in the Midwest. The East and West of America, to use my words, are more interested in self-expression, in the search for the white stone.

But it is also possible to use the categories as dimensions of our personal development. Maslow, the American psychologist on whose work these categories are based, insisted that the categories nest inside each other, like Chinese boxes. We are never completely one or the other, and it is a mix which changes at different times throughout life. I can well recognize periods when I was largely sustenance driven concerned with my very survival at the start of my career. Then came the period of achievement in very worldly terms, when I was concerned about proving myself. I still find myself casting envious glances at the smart houses advertised for sale in the glossy magazines, so I am not at all immune from the symbols of success of the outer-directed world. I like to think, however, that now, well into my third age, I am anchored in the values of the inner-directed group and searching for a way to express my real self and to make a contribution of some sort.

To say this implies that there is a ladder of progression from sustenance driven, through the outer directed, to the inner directed. This would be consistent with the teaching of people like Maslow and other developmental psychologists, and it rings true of the experience of many people as they progress through life. If we want control over our own destinies, which, I am arguing, is the only choice we have, then we would be foolish to make our wishes subject to the fashions of others, which is what drives both of the first two dimensions. We would be well advised to shift as quickly as we can to a view of life which is predominantly inner directed.

I recognize, however, that this is asking a lot of people who have never tasted the freedom that comes with this state of mind, nor is it easy to enjoy the inner-directed life without first embracing large chunks of the first two dimensions. Yet to say, as some do, that inner direction, or self-expression and the control of your own life, is only possible for middle-class, middle-income, and middle-aged individuals is to be ridiculously patronizing. The young and the poor may not find it easy, but to allocate them automatically to the ranks of the sustenance driven is to assume that they have no wish to be responsible for their own future, however difficult that might be.

Who, then, are all these inner-directed ones? If over one third of major regions of America fall into this category it seems strange that we do not hear more of them and from them. That remains the challenge—to carry a proper selfishness into the public domain. It is an issue addressed in the third part of this book. It is probable, however, that the inner-directed or properly selfish ones have quieter voices than the outer-directed ones, and so receive less attention. The noise of the public debate may conceal a more private simplicity. Edmund Burke once said, two hundred years ago:

> Because half a dozen grasshoppers under a fern make the field ring with their importunate clink, while thousands of great cattle, reposed beneath the shadow of the British oak, chew the cud and are silent, pray do not imagine that those who make the noise are the only inhabitants of the field, that they are many in number, or that, after all, they are anything other than little, shriveling, meager, hopping, though loud and troublesome, insects of the hour.

Caught up in the rhetoric of the material age, we may hear only the grasshoppers. We should listen more carefully to the quieter sounds.

THE MORALITY OF SELFISHNESS

Selfishness at its worst is individualism carried to extremes, unconcerned and intolerant of others. Proper selfishness spreads beyond oneself. It is properly moral, in the sense in which Kant, the great German philosopher, understood morality. Kant held that we were all born with a moral impulse but that we had to work out for ourselves what that meant in practice. His rule was that whatever you felt was right for you must also be right for everyone else. If I can steal your property, annoy you by my intemperate behavior—or disobey the laws if it suits me, then so can you, and I shouldn't complain. There should not be one code for the rich and another for the poor. Morality, in other words, starts with oneself, but has to work for everyone else too.

If one thinks about this long enough and hard enough some

sort of recipe for a decent society will emerge. The process starts with ourselves, and is progressively moderated as the impact of what would be right for us is extended to everyone else. In the end some approximate definition of justice, of what is fair, emerges. Were schools to give Kant's exercise to their students it might be the most effective way of helping them to understand what morals mean in practice, instead of asking them to accept what was handed down to them by their elders. My own experience suggests that Kant is right and that there is an innate sense of justice, or a moral impulse, in all of us, even the very young, and that it is not difficult for them to agree on some fundamental principles of right and wrong if the question, not our answers, is put to them.

We should not imagine, however, that the pursuit of proper selfishness is a purely rational process. We must also listen to our emotions and our instincts if we are going to be really true to ourselves. In his book, *Descartes' Error*, Antonio Damasio describes twelve patients who lost the prefrontal part of their brains, the part which controls our emotions. These people were "rational fools." They were normal in every respect, had no paralysis and no damage to their general intelligence, and performed just as well in psychological tests as they did before their accidents. But their lives seemed to fall apart. They could not hold down jobs, show affection, or take decisions. They were completely cold-blooded, showing no response to either good news or bad, to love or to hate. Despite their rationality, they had lost control of their lives, were no longer hungry for the truth about themselves, and could no longer be properly selfish.

One of the worst aspects of some business studies courses is the assumption that business people are rational fools, devoid of emotion or any sense of responsibility. I have known such people. They are hard to deal with because they have no conscience, regard concepts such as loyalty or trust as wimpish and suspect, look only at the numbers, and care only for themselves. They sometimes die rich, but always friendless. Thankfully they are rare in most businesses. We should not encourage them.

Attach too much importance to rationality, or attribute too much to our genes, and altruism will become a meaningless concept, something which has always been the worry of rational economists. Robert Frank, one economist who has tried to integrate economics and biology, has said that "Adam Smith's carrot and Darwin's stick have by now rendered character development a completely forgotten theme in many industrialized countries." Since character, and its development, is the essence of proper selfishness, we must be careful not to make the same mistake. Frank's argument is that altruism, or acts of genuine goodness, are the price we pay for having moral sentiments. It is possible, of course, to argue that giving blood, for instance, or coins to beggars, or volunteering for relief work, are rational acts even though there is no obvious payoff, because they make us feel good about ourselves. But, more benevolently, it may be that acts of true generosity are aspects of ourselves revealed in action. Proper selfishness would want to see as many of those aspects revealed as possible.

We have long been urged to "love thy neighbor as thyself." For many neighbors this could be rather bad news, since few of us have much love for ourselves. The first part of a proper selfishness, therefore, is a readiness to come to terms with ourselves as we are, and to move ourselves towards what we would like to be. Only when we are comfortable in our own skins will we be of much use to anyone else. A decent society has, annoyingly perhaps, to start with us, with each one of us, and with what we, individually, believe we could be, and what we believe a decent society ought to look like.

This sounds like hard work. It would be more convenient if others did the philosophizing for us. Isn't that, some may say, what we pay governments for? But that is to misunderstand democracy. Democracy assumes that individuals must be allowed to be the best judge of their own interests, even if they often seem to be misguided. Governments are not there to tell us what to believe or think, they are there to represent our beliefs, and to translate them into laws or regulations. Socrates also sought the meaning of truth, justice, beauty, and the decent society, but he did it by questioning people about how they understood those words. It is inadequate to borrow beliefs. We have to work them out for ourselves.

May 2, 1997, was a beautiful sun-drenched day in Britain. A strange excitement was around. A government had changed. A sense of new possibilities filled the air. Even those who had not voted for Tony Blair's new government could scarce help responding to the mood of the moment. Strangely, the election had not been about economics, which the previous, Conservative, government had managed rather well, nor about policies, which were almost identical in every manifesto. Economics mattered, of course, but what mattered more was what sort of country and what sort of government the people wanted. The new government guessed it right. "We are the servants now," insisted the new prime minister.

When the people know what they feel about life and society, governments would have no choice but to respond. If we sit silent only Edmund Burke's grasshoppers will be heard.

The Search for Meaning

THE SEARCH for the best in ourselves is only the beginning. We need a purpose for these selves.

There is, first, the elusive question of where we are heading,
of what success might mean. Nietzsche said that those who have
a *why* can endure any *how*, but it is the *why* that is difficult. The
mother of the child with cerebral palsy could testify to the truth
of that. We all need a "telos," a dream of what might be, to give
us energy for the journey.

Secondly, there is the paradoxical doctrine of "Enough." You
cannot move on to a different track unless you realize that you
have gone far enough on the present one. If you don't know what
enough is, in material or achievement terms, you are trapped in a
rut of your own devising and will never learn what might be
outside that rut.

Thirdly, we all need a taste of the sublime, to lift our hearts,
to give us a hint of something bigger than ourselves and of the

infinite possibilities of life. The Department of Education in Britain sums it up rather well, in their official definition of spirituality: "The valuing of the non-material aspects of life, and intimations of an enduring reality."

Fourthly, and lastly, there is the challenge of immortality. No, we can't live forever, at least in this world, and we can't take anything with us, but we can leave a bit of ourselves behind, as proof that we made a difference, to someone. That only happens, I believe, by concentrating on others, the ultimate paradox of proper selfishness.

Put the four elements together and you have a reason for living, even though it does end up as a perpetual quest, with an uncertain ending. The journey is the point, not the arrival. To settle for anything less is to accept that one is content to be a happy cabbage.

I will argue, later, that these four requirements apply to institutions and to businesses as much as they do to individuals, but our first concern is properly with ourselves.

THE DREAM

At one time, I was under considerable stress. Work was difficult and that meant less time and energy for my family or for other interests, which created yet more problems. After some persuasion I went to a psychotherapist. He asked me what I was trying to do with my life. A good question, and one I was ready for. With appropriate humility I said that I was trying to improve the world a little bit, through my work. "Ah!" he said, "that's wonderful, so now we have this grand quartet—Jesus Christ, Mohammed, Karl Marx . . . and Charles Handy." I was indignant that I should be paying good money for this mockery from someone who was supposed to be on my side. It took a week or two, but when I quieted down, I eventually realized that he was telling me that if you want to change the world you have to start with your own life. As the aborigines in Australia put it, "You must become the change you want to see in the world."

There is a passage in the Gospel of Thomas, one of the unofficial Gnostic Gospels which you won't find in the Bible. It goes like this: "If you bring forth what is within you, what you bring forth will save you. If you do not bring forth what is within you, then what you do not bring forth will destroy you." To that add a remark by the director of the Boston Fine Arts Museum. He said, "We used to think that it was a special sort of person who became an artist or an actor or whatever. Now I think that's wrong. I think that every person is an artist in some way." We don't have to change the world; it is challenge enough to live up to our dream of what kind of person we could be. That, in itself, will make a difference. I also like the Japanese idea that life is a game, not a trivial child's game, but a serious game, a challenge. It is our job to excel in this game of life with whatever skill or expertise we have.

I can't say that I find it easy to walk my own talk. I come from a long line of preachers, and preaching comes more easily to me than practicing, but a part of life is crossing things off a list, until you are left with what is real and genuine at last. As Michelangelo said, the perfect form lies concealed in the block of stone; all that is needed is to chip away until it is revealed. I was fortunate. I got some things out of my system early on. Posted by my company to what had been an outpost of the old British Empire, I was the manager of a sales company in Sarawak in my twenties—my own command. I also lived what was, by the standards of my vicarage upbringing, a life of luxury, with servants, chauffeur, and even an armed sentry at night. These people were all paid by the company. I had no personal wealth but all the appurtenances of wealth at an indecently early age.

Needless to say, I am now deeply ashamed of all that self-indulgence in a country that was, at that time, poor but proud. It was, however, a chance to indulge all my more materialistic needs, and, thereafter, to begin to move on, first from a state of sustenance (I began to have confidence that I would survive) to an outer-directed life, where I could pursue achievement in different fields, and finally to one more inner directed. The material things that some hope to find towards the end of their working life, I chanced upon early in my career. Three years later I was back in London on promotion, but, no longer enjoying my overseas allowances, I was living in a basement flat, unable to pay the gas bill.

The dream later changed, after the death of my father. I realized that to be truly worthwhile it had to be directed beyond myself, and had to be decently modest in ambition if it was to be fulfilled. These days, as I revisit my life in my sixties, I would settle for Ralph Waldo Emerson's definition of success:

> To laugh often and much; to win the respect of intelligent people and the affection of children; to earn the appreciation of honest critics and to endure the betrayal of false friends; to appreciate beauty; to find the best in others; to leave the world a bit better, whether by a healthy child, a garden patch, or a redeemed social condition; to know that even one life has breathed easier because you lived; this is to have succeeded.

Too pious? Maybe. And I still have those occasional worries about survival and the desires for public recognition which go with sustenance and outer-directed values. But maybe we underestimate the simple decency of most people's ambitions. I first came across Emerson's words in a small art gallery in the back streets of Mumbai, which used to be called Bombay. I was struck how something written more than a century ago can still find resonance in parts, at least, of both old India and modern America. When a magazine such as *American Benefactor* can have the success that it has had in its initial launch we have to ask whether we are not witnessing a change in the prevailing culture of rich America. It may be that those who used to define themselves through conspicuous consumption are now finding their identity by giving time and money to others. "Downshifting" is no longer a term of abuse but something that many genuinely aspire to, as they realize that the pursuit of conventional success has squeezed out all the time for other things. It is those "other things" that many now yearn for and are content to be judged by.

Our dream for ourselves is not entirely rational. It is certainly not defined only in monetary terms, as we have seen, even though money is often a means of recognition, not just a way of satisfying material needs. Entrepreneurs don't want their millions because they need to buy things with them; they want them because they are the outward sign of their success in venturing, in adding new value to the world. Top professionals don't physically need all the money they can earn; they want it to show how successful they are. They want the recognition that they have been an artist in their own way in the great game of life.

Rationality doesn't explain our occasional willingness to fight for those we hold dear, be they people or causes—our impetuous leap into a river to save a drowning child, a lifetime of dedication to helping incurables, or a desire to work among the poor for little thanks and no public recognition. Yet, for some, these actions or callings are the stuff of their lives, and we should be grateful that it is so. The heart has its reasons, said Pascal, which reason knows not of. There is no universal criterion for success or for individual dreams. For each their own, and hence the hunger.

For many years I used the obituary exercise. I worked out, from medical tables, that unless I met with accident or abused my body too much, I was statistically likely to live to the age of seventy-seven. I then composed the short memorial address that I should ideally like to be given at my funeral by one of my oldest and best friends. This sort of exercise forces you to look back on your life and pick out the things of which you are most proud. It is a way of focusing on your dream. The exercise, after a time, became too familiar. It had served its purpose. These days I keep a sealed envelope with a letter to my two children to be read by them after my death. I try to review it every year. In it I find myself spelling out the values by which I have tried to live my life, and my hopes for them. It is another way of creating the talk which I must then try to walk.

THE DOCTRINE OF ENOUGH

"Roses need pruning if they are to flower," a friend replied when I complained of being overstretched. With great reluctance, because I was enjoying the spread of my activities, although conscious that nothing much was coming out of them all, I resigned from seven different committees and groups on the same day. Only two of them replied to my resignation letter. Obviously the rest did not notice, or mind, whether I was there or not. It was my first introduction to the doctrine of "enough," or what we might, more elegantly, call a decent sufficiency, or, more academically, a theory of limits.

In most of life we can recognize "enough." We know when we have had enough to eat, when the heating or the air conditioning is enough, when we have had enough sleep or done enough preparation. More than enough is then unnecessary, and can even be counterproductive. We could, with advantage, recognize when the level of enough has been reached in other fields. Those who do not know what enough is cannot move on. They do not explore new worlds, they do not learn, they grow only in one dimension. They are, I believe, unlikely to earn their white stone. They are trapped in the rut of their own success, always wanting more of the same, always dissatisfied, never knowing the feeling of abundance. Asked what enough was, John D. Rockefeller replied, "Just one more!" In this philosophy more is not necessarily better. We have to travel what the ancients called the *via negativa*. We have to learn to say "no" in order to move on. Arguably, in fact, the lower you define your level of enough, the sooner you will taste abundance and the freer you will be.

On the other hand, in another sense, enough is never enough. I remember being chided by my teacher after one examination.

"That was a poor performance," he said, "I expected more of you."

"I passed, didn't I?" I replied indignantly. "Isn't that good enough?"

"But you could have done better. Enough is never enough where your personal standards are involved. You let yourself down."

Personal growth, the search for the white stone, has no limits. Everything else does.

Growth does not have to mean more of the same. It can mean better rather than bigger. It can mean leaner or deeper, both of which might improve rather than expand the current position. Businesses can grow more profitable by becoming better, or leaner, or deeper, more concentrated, without growing bigger. Bigness, in both business and life, can lead to a lack of focus, too much complexity and, in the end, too wide a spread to control. We have to know when big is big enough.

Businesses, for instance, which aim to match or exceed last year's growth rate give themselves a harder task each year: 10 percent this year is the equivalent of 11 percent last year. Like Sisyphus, in the Greek myth, no matter how hard they push the stone they will never get to the top of the hill. Even if they do, they will by then be so large that they will be dismembered, by choice or force, and will have to start all over again. Look at ICI or Hanson in the UK, both of which grew only to split when they got too big. There is an alternative. Once big enough they can grow better, not bigger. It is a formula which Germany's *mittelstander*, their small family firms, have tried and tested to great advantage, content to corner and dominate one small niche market, through constant improvement and innovation. Rich enough, and big enough, they concentrate on the pursuit of excellence, for its own sake as much as anything.

Society, too, has the same choice—bigger or better. We could choose to trade off some efficiency in exchange for more fairness, because the other side of the philosophy of enough is the right of everyone to taste the possibility of enough. Take Japan, where some domestic industries, such as gasoline sales, are rigorously price controlled. The companies are forced to compete on service, not price, which is kept high. The result is that a visit to a service station in Japan is like a visit to a beauty parlor with attendants swarming all over the car. Compare that to the price-competitive, cost-efficient world of the West where you usually have to fill your own vehicle, where to make the customer do the work is seen as smart business, and where any young people to be seen are more likely to rob you than to help you, being unemployed, envious, and resentful. Yet we still pay for these young people, through our taxes.

Many would prefer the Japanese way, which recognizes that there can be proper limits to price competition in the interest of a decent society. Better, not richer. We can't do it in our export industries but we could in the domestic sphere, and we certainly could in the public sector. Higher prices domestically but more jobs seems a reasonable trade-off for a fair society, but one that runs against conventional wisdom, which argues in favor of lower costs, and prices, to make more jobs. Japan has recently changed her mind and decided to deregulate her domestic economy in order to stimulate growth. We might predict that more unemployment, envy, and violence will soon be seen in Japan as more people lose the chance of defining their own level of enough.

More broadly, a society that does not recognize the morality of "enough" will see excesses arise which verge on the obscene, as those who have first choice of society's riches appropriate them for themselves. Democracy will not long tolerate such an abuse of the market. We are, as I have already observed, in the midst of what has been called the ascendancy of the professionals. Historically, in the Agrarian Revolution, our hunter-gatherer ancestors were replaced by a land-owning class, who were, in turn, replaced in the Industrial Revolution by the owners of the mills and the factories. In each case, it was the self-indulgence of the current ruling class that ultimately led to their replacement. The professionals of today—a classification which includes top managers, consultants, and financiers as well as lawyers, doctors, and members of other older professions—need to be aware of the danger. It was Edmund Burke who said, "Men are qualified for civil liberty in exact proportion to their disposition to put moral chains upon their own appetites."

When senior executives of companies earn fifty, sometimes even one hundred, times the pay of their own workers, it is hard not to feel that it is an affront to those workers. The executives compare their exotic salaries and benefits to the rewards given to the stars of sports or films or music, but these have earned their rewards by their own individual efforts, whereas the executives are supposed to be members of a team. Would the team, one often wonders, do so much worse if that particular player was absent?

"I couldn't run my company on the basis of this doctrine of enough," one chief executive told me. "No one would want to work there." I could not help replying that if material greed was the main basis for people choosing to join his company it must be a very uninspiring place. Money is sometimes a substitute for other things.

The philosophy of "enough" cannot be imposed on a society. It is a matter of norms, not laws. But norms are set by the elite, whose example sets the fashion. What the top does today, the middle imitates tomorrow, and the bottom aspires to, some day. Noblesse oblige, as always, but laws can help to nudge the noblesse in the right direction. A progressive consumption tax, for instance, which taxes expenditure not income, but which increases with the price of the goods, would make conspicuous consumption too expensive to be worth it, while keeping cheap things cheap. Alternatively, a tax regime which permits top salaries to be tax deductible only up to a certain limit, would make some of today's executive remuneration packages more obviously a theft of shareholders' funds. But laws only work if they reinforce what society feels to be right. There is, in the end, no way that laws can substitute for values.

I have always been interested in the old idea of the stipendiary principle. This principle, originally adopted by religious organizations, seeks to guarantee their people enough to live on, leaving them free of worry about their material needs and, therefore, free to concentrate on their real work, their calling or vocation. It is a principle that at one time used to apply to all public servants in Britain, including politicians, but which has long since become eroded, partly because inflation mucked up the calculations and partly because people started comparing the standards of "enough" across occupational groups, thereby effectively entering the market society with all its implications for a change in the measuring stick. My father, as a country parson, lived on a stipend. We weren't rich, but we never starved. Money was never the measure of anything he did and his life was the freer for it.

We are, however, free to adopt our own version of the stipendiary principle in our own lives. My wife and I, since we became self-employed portfolio people, have regularly sat down each year and worked out what we need to live on. Since our standards of comfort and future financial security are quite high so are our levels of "enough." Many would envy them, and they are certainly not monastic. But, regardless of the level, the simple act of doing this removes the temptation to maximize our income by working around the clock and the calendar, which is the dilemma of every self-employed person, because who knows where the next order is coming from. The process has freed up a lot of our time, because once the "enough" is guaranteed, there is no need or desire to spend time on making more than enough.

More activity is, then, only justified if it is valuable for its own sake. One can even give the activity away, for free, without feeling any sense of self-denial. Easy virtue. I now realize, in my own life, how even more free I would be if I could bring myself to set the level of "enough" ever lower each year, and if I could say "no" more often, but the *via negativa* is a hard road. Market economists might disapprove or disbelieve, but the stipendiary principle does set us free to do what we are meant to do. We don't have to be hair-shirted about it. An "elegant sufficiency" is a more comfortable concept than a stipend, and still consistent with the doctrine of enough.

It is, of course, easy to say that enough is enough when you quite clearly already have enough. The problem for most people is getting to that stage. A society which adopts the doctrine of enough has to make it a priority to ensure that everyone has a real chance of being able to reach their personal level of enough, so that they can move on. No one can say what that level should be for anyone else. It has to be a personal decision. It need not, however, be related to anyone else. What one person might think was not enough, another might consider more than enough. It depends on a trade-off of risks: the risk of moving on, and, perhaps, of failing, against the risk of missing out on a new opportunity, a new chance to learn. The lower one can set the level of enough the freer one is to explore something else. It is that freedom which we should want everyone to have.

The Puritan denial of materialism, their philosophy of make do and mend, rather than throw away and buy another, forced them to cultivate the virtues of honesty and thrift, which actually made their societies rich and, in many respects, more equal. We might try their ways again and see what happens. If the philosophy of enough reduced the level of envy in society even by a little, that could not be bad. If it then redirected some of our energies to making and doing rather than mere getting and spending it would be better still.

Recently, I had the unique experience of staying for a week on Norfolk Island. Nothing to do with the English Norfolk, this is a tiny island in the South Pacific, two hours' flying time from both New Zealand and Australia, with 1,500 inhabitants. It is hard to get there, and, with its cliffs and coral reefs, harder still to land anything there. It is a very self-sufficient little place, proudly independent although an Australian protectorate, with a modest income from the tourists who fly in on the six or seven flights a week.

With no income tax the island attracts two or three millionaires but, paradoxically, money is of little value because there is nothing much to buy. As a result, theft and burglary have little point. No one locks their doors, cars are hardly needed on an island that is only five miles long and three miles wide, and those cars that do exist are battered boxes on wheels which is all that is required. Status doesn't carry much weight on an island where everyone knows everyone and where most people are related. People do just enough work to provide the means of existence, because there is not much point in doing more. It is an island where the philosophy of enough is taken seriously. The climate is fine and warm and the beaches are beautiful. "Being" not "getting" or "having" or even "doing" is what it's all about. It was bliss for a week.

But, thinking about it, I have to confess that the idea of living there all the time was profoundly disturbing. Without all the conventional measures of success I was not sure that I would know what to do with myself. "Being" could become "decaying." The challenge to grow and develop without any pressures or even opportunities to prove myself might be too difficult. The doctrine of enough does not mean giving up or renouncing all the activities of this world. It is hard, if not impossible, to "be" without "doing." The doctrine requires that we move on, not that we withdraw, that we recognize when more of something no longer means personal growth. Most of us cling too long to the comfortable and the familiar.

A TASTE OF THE SUBLIME

Life can be a trudge, working to eat and eating to work—for what? I need, we all need, the occasional reminder that the world is an extraordinary place and that people are capable of extraordinary things.

A poverty of aspiration—a hurtful but true criticism of much of Britain after the war, and of many inner-city areas in America today—can be fatal to a continuing exploration of all the possibilities in life. Enough can mean full stop, rather than a springboard for something new, unless imagination is stirred, senses aroused, and ideas and questions kindled. Nature at its best, animals in the wild, the starry skies above, said Kant, that stern philosopher; but also man-made things and occasions, the arts in all their forms, festivals and feasts, acts of great generosity and courage, of love and sacrifice—such things can all provide us with a glimpse of excellence and a taste of the sublime. God, said Dame Julian of Norwich, is in everything that is good, and God is in each one of us. If God be another word for The Good, then to find the good in ourselves we need first to look for it in the good things of the world, not least to remind ourselves that there *is* good out there, and therefore, most likely in ourselves. Sad must be those who never see it.

St. Petersburg in winter is a magnificent but uncomfortable place. It is cold, grey, wet, and gloomy, or can be in November, which is when I was last there. The Russian people whom I met were likewise grey and gloomy. Capitalism has not had the rejuvenating effect in St. Petersburg that it has had in parts of Eastern Europe, and perhaps in some other parts of Russia. There is nothing much in the shops, and few have the wherewithal with which to buy what there is. If I were a St. Petersburger in the winter I would be inclined to wonder what life was all about, and whether any of it was worth it.

Until, that is, I went to the Mariinsky Theater to see the *Nutcracker Suite* ballet. This theater is a magnificent place, a green and gold extravaganza—and packed with people. The most expensive tickets, for Russians, were less than $5 (still dear for them) but most were much less. Whole families were there, as were school classes with their teachers, young and old alike, some smart, some shabby, all agog.

The ballet is unashamedly romantic, and the last act a fantasy of a ballet lover's heaven. Even the most cynical could not help but be stirred by its beauty, particularly when danced tradition-ally but to perfection by the Kirov School. I went out into the cold night wondering about the contradictions—the poverty and inefficiency outside and the sumptuous excellence inside. Was this the Russian version of bread and circuses, a way to pacify the mob, to make up for all their hardships; or do the Russians see the arts as a glimpse of the transcendent, something that will help us make sense of life, and therefore to be made available to all, as cheaply as possible?

Looking at the rapt faces of the audience that night and watching the crowds of ordinary Russians pouring into the Her-mitage the next day, with its unbeatable collection of paintings, I am inclined to the more elevated view. These people weren't there just to get out of the cold, they were coming to see some things that were near to the sublime and the eternal. If they went away uplifted for a while, or pondering on the real meaning of life, of what endured and what was passing fancy, surely this was no bad thing. If the evening gave them the impulse to rise above their present condition, surely even better.

It will be interesting to see whether the Mariinsky Theater

and the Kirov Ballet survive when Russia eventually embraces the free market. Put art of this quality into the marketplace, with realistic costs and prices, and it inevitably becomes expensive, a playground for the rich. Too bad, then, if you are poor and can't get your own taste of truth and beauty from the great theaters, concert halls, or museums. The market, one has to conclude, is not always the best guarantee of free choice or democracy.

Yet, paradoxically, for the market to work in the sectors where it does work well, we need to know that there is more to life than marketplace success. Those who struggle unsuccessfully in that marketplace will better tolerate the riches of the successful if they realize that there are some things that money cannot buy. The arts in their many different guises offer some hint of that other, deeper world. Art, said Picasso, blows away the everyday cobwebs from the soul. All should have the chance to taste that breeze. Market economy or not, some things perhaps should not be priced too high, so that they are available to all.

In Italy, four years ago, the workers throughout Tuscany went on strike for a day—in protest at the bomb which destroyed a part of the Uffizi Gallery in Florence. It is hard to imagine the people of New York or London doing the same, but to the people of Tuscany their art is their heritage; it enriches their everyday life. They are fortunate—they see it all around them every day, in the architecture and sculptures of their cities, in the frescoes which still embellish the walls of their churches. In summer, their towns are full of music. Most of it is there for free.

We speak, in most of America and Europe, of education and health care as the entitlements of every citizen in what we would like to think of as our civilized societies. In a truly civilized society, that entitlement would include open access to all the things that stir our imaginations. If we can't put those things in our streets, we should let the people through the doors. It would compensate a little for the inefficiencies that are inevitable in any free enterprise system, and would permit more tolerance, encourage more creativity, and release more talent. It might even turn out to be a good market investment for the nation.

Most of all, however, the arts put the rest of our life in perspective. At peak moments they help to move us on, to make the struggle seem worthwhile. That happened for me one summer in Spoleto. Forty years ago, Gian-Carlo Menotti, looking for a small town in which to stage a festival of music and theater in his native Italy, settled on this beautiful but previously unnoticed place in Southern Umbria. Today, the three weeks of the Spoleto Festival attract distinguished musicians and performers from all over the world, and the little town hums with music and the arts under the summer sun. Conviviality is in the air. It is good to be alive, and to be there.

The climax is the final "Concerto in Piazza," staged in front of the magnificent cathedral, with an audience of some six thousand seated in the piazza and stretching way up the long flight of steps behind. That year they performed Mahler's Resurrection Symphony, all one and a half hours of it, complete with choir, and trumpeters on the balcony, on a balmy night, with Menotti, then eighty-five, there to introduce it. Magic, of a sort, even if the gold-bedangled part of the audience had clearly come from Rome more to be seen than to listen. But there was, to this listener anyway, a message behind the magic.

Writing about this symphony, Mahler observed that each of us must, at some time, question what it is all for. Is life just a scherzo, he asked, to be rattled through as quickly and harmoniously as possible? Or is there more to it? I will answer that question, he said, in the final movement. That movement is an exciting, upsetting, and at the same time, uplifting piece of music. I listened to it once, on my headphones, on a plane coming back to Britain over the Atlantic, as dawn was breaking above the clouds, when nature and the music seemed in complete harmony. It was even more powerful in Spoleto.

Each must make his own interpretation of what Mahler was trying to say in that last movement. For me, it was a declaration that, for all its ups and downs, life is about more than surviving—there could be something glorious about it, it could contribute to a better world. That leaves one with a personal challenge, to do something glorious with one's life. It is also, I believe, a challenge for every organization and every business that has, in effect, bought large chunks of other people's lives. It is not enough to offer a scherzo.

The Kirov Ballet and Mahler in Spoleto sound splendidly elitist. They happen to tingle my own imagination more than a pop concert. To each his own. For me, too, a good play in the theater is a form of highlighter, emphasizing aspects of life which need to be thought about. Others find that different perspective in films or novels. Nor does one have to be rich or privileged to provide others with a hint of greater things, to make something glorious. Alan Bennett, the British playwright, recounts in one of his essays how as a young lad he used to go to the symphony concerts in Leeds and ride home on the tram afterwards along with several of the musicians "who would sit there, rather shabby and ordinary, and often with fag ends in their mouths, worlds away from the Delius, Walton and Brahms they had been playing. It was a first lesson to me that . . . ordinary middle-aged men in raincoats can be instruments of the sublime."

"Instruments of the sublime." Yes, indeed—ordinary people can always raise the world a notch or two for those around them, creating another sort of feel-good factor. And it doesn't have to be in concert halls—it can happen in our own families, where life can often mean just getting through the day, or at work, where work can be a boring four-letter word instead of the creative, exciting thing it's meant to be. And it doesn't need money. It's an attitude of mind. Elizabeth, in her work as a portrait photographer, unusually I think, sets out to make portraits that encourage people to feel good about themselves, to show what is best in them. It can change their lives. We can all do something to stimulate someone's imagination. It is, in fact, I believe, not only our privilege to be an instrument of the sublime, but our responsibility, and it's a lot more fun than looking at a bank statement and wondering if that is all there is to life.

A SORT OF IMMORTALITY

Unless you believe in reincarnation, it is not given to us humans to see more than one life on this earth, but it is possible to leave some imprint of yourself behind, thus achieving a sort of immortality, although one to be enjoyed by others, not ourselves. It is an idea captured in that most poignant of military memorial inscriptions: "For your tomorrow, we gave our today." Leaving an imprint does not have to be this sacrificial, thank God. Gifts of ourselves take many forms, but they are all unique.

Maybe, I reflected in that piazza in Spoleto, Mahler was hinting that if we are to deserve some sort of immortality, even to contemplate the notion that we have left an indelible mark on time, then we have to aspire to be something special, to change and grow. We live on in others, thereby. For many, the children that they rear are their best legacy, their enduring gift to humanity. For others it is the work they do, or the businesses they create. For some it is the lives they saved or bettered, the kids they taught or the sick they healed. The sobering thought is that individuals and societies are not, in the end, remembered for how they made their money, but for how they spent it. A headstone in the graveyard that records the millions made by the body buried there impresses none of the passers-by. It is what was done with the millions that counts. The imprint we leave on the world is the only form of temporary immortality of which we can be sure. In the end, that is where we find our true identity. Anything else is only a step upon the ladder. A person who recognizes this will understand that "enough" is an invitation to climb higher on the ladder, and a society which buys into the contribution ethic will use capitalism as its tool and not its purpose.

Some contributions come early in life, some much later. We can take comfort from Degas, who painted his most enchanting portraits after most people's normal retirement age. These works all came about because he felt a failure. When he hit sixty, Degas looked back at his life and work and decided that it amounted to nothing. The vogue for his impressionist art seemed to have passed, and now it all seemed to him a flash in the pan, a waste of paint. He turned his back on life and retreated to his dark brown studio, determined to create, at last, something special, not for anyone else to see or buy, just for himself. He died at eighty-three, evicted from his studio, blind, lonely, and depressed. Only now can we see, for the first time, the full, glorious fruits of his last twenty years.

You don't have to be sixty and a temperamental artist to look back at your life and wonder if it wasn't all chaff in the wind. From time to time I take out my old appointment diaries and wonder who all those people were that I was meeting, what those committees were all about, and what, if anything, we achieved. Nelson Mandela has seen *his* life's work fully justified, but he says in his autobiography that he wondered at times, during those dark prison years, whether he might not have done better to have been an ordinary lawyer, at home with his wife and family.

But it is not for us to judge our own lives. Nor can we necessarily expect any judgment in our own lifetime. Degas would have been astounded to see the admiring crowds around his late-life pictures. His work inspires us, as does his example. Cathedrals also inspire. It is not only their grandeur or splendor, but the thought that they often took more than fifty years to build. Those who designed them, those who first worked on them, knew for certain that they would never see them finished. They knew only that they were creating something glorious which would stand for centuries, long after their own names had been forgotten. They had their own dream of the sublime and of immortality. We may not need any more cathedrals but we do need cathedral thinkers, people who can think beyond their own lifetimes.

SEVEN

The Necessity of Others

I KEEP ON my desk a reproduction of Van Gogh's painting *Irises*. Set amid a group of vivid blue irises, he has painted one white iris. "That's me," I thought when I first saw it, "the lonely one in a crowd, the different one." I now see it as a symbol of proper selfishness, the distinct and different iris, certainly, but still an iris, part of something bigger and gaining a large part of its identity from the others around it. By itself the white iris would have little meaning; it is because it is part of, yet different from, the surrounding group that it has significance. "I" needs "We" to be truly "I" as Jung put it. It can only be disturbing, therefore, that a recent survey showed that 63 percent of Americans declared themselves unconcerned with others. They may be missing something.

True individualism is necessarily social, I have argued. It isn't obvious, however, what "social" implies or what our relations are or should be to our fellow citizens. It is a question that has troubled people for thousands of years, because our relationship to the rest of the world lies at the heart of all moral and ethical questions. Right and wrong are ideas which are only necessary because other people impinge on us and we on them. We cannot know how we should behave unless we know what our connection is to other people. To Aristotle and Confucius it was obvious. We come into the world as part of something bigger, a family, a community, a nation. Like it or not we have obligations to them. More than that, to be fully ourselves we need them, for how can you be good, or kind, or virtuous if there is no one else around to practise these virtues on? A totally self-sufficient human being could only be some sort of god. Not being gods, we need other people in order to be ourselves.

There is everyday evidence to support the ancients. Altruism and generosity; sympathy, kindness, and selflessness—all the things we prize and admire in people whom we hold to be good are to do with promoting the good of others. Why do people scrimp and save to give their children a better deal in life? Why give money to a beggar if he or she isn't threatening you, or tip a waiter if you won't be going back to that restaurant again? Yet we do all these things, and more, things which are hard to justify by any rationality other than our empathy with others. Morality stems from empathy, some say. It is even suggested that it is our ability to empathize with the plight of others that distinguishes us as humans. Deeds done for others bring out the best in us.

The individualism of the West started from another base. Man, said Hobbes, is born only with the basic right to defend himself or herself. Everything else is up for debate. It makes good sense, however, to accept a basic contract with society in which one undertakes to obey certain rules, as long as others do so as well, because otherwise one would be perpetually fighting to stay alive, the original state of nature. Our relations with other people, therefore, even with our families, once we are old enough to think for ourselves, are matters of contract, of mutual agreement. Although these have been worked on by preceding generations, there is always the possibility of renegotiation. This tradition starts with our rights, not our obligations, nor our feelings of empathy.

We need to make up our minds about which of these two traditions we believe, because we live and work with others all our lives. It is through our interaction with them that we grow or fail to grow. Life can be a self-fulfilling prophecy. If you believe people to be untrustworthy, devious, and concerned only for themselves, as did Hobbes, they will often prove you right and you will behave that way yourself. If you believe them to be essentially decent they, and you, may live up to your expectations. Proper selfishness requires that we side with the Greeks, while recognizing, to be realistic, that some others may be Hobbesians.

The question gets more urgent as we all get more interconnected. Almost everything we do affects other people, whether it is the pollution from our car or our decision to buy one computer rather than another. National boundaries can't control the winds that carry acid rain, the flows of money, or the messages on the Internet. In no way can we stand alone and pretend that what we do affects no one else and that no one else affects us.

"Connexity" is the word that Geoff Mulgan of Demos has coined for this new age, arguing that the big question of our times is whether we can combine the freedom and opportunities which are thrown open to us with the necessity for interdependence. Or are we doomed, he asks, to a classical tragedy in which our love of freedom destroys our capacity to be interdependent? George Soros, billionaire financier, put it this way in his critique of capitalism in the *Atlantic Monthly:* "Unless it [the uninhibited pursuit of self-interest] is tempered by the recognition of a commitment that ought to take precedence over particular interests, our present system is liable to break down."

Maybe all we need is a little encouragement to give expression to the more creative and altruistic sides of our natures. Yes, our genes are selfish, in that they seek their own perpetuation, but, in order to do that, those selfish genes may encourage their owners to make sacrifices for their kin, even to die for them, so that the inheritance survives. These selfish genes also recognize that it makes sense to do good for one's neighbor as long as the deed is reciprocated—what is termed mutual altruism.

We can see the evidence in our own behavior if we stand back and look at ourselves. We make sacrifices for our children, and we are prepared to fight and even die for causes which have no immediate or direct payoff for ourselves. We don't do the logical thing and push old people into holes in the ground once they have ceased to contribute. We don't kill off the maimed and the diseased or the useless, even though they cost us all some of our money. We don't, it seems, want to live in that sort of society, if only because what is done to others might one day be done to us or ours. A proper selfishness would see the sense in investing in others in order to create a better world for our descendants. Setting limits to our own needs, defining what is enough, leaves more room to attend to the needs of others, to our own ultimate benefit. The fact that it is part of our human nature to do this should encourage us. The mixture of self-interest and altruism can be a powerful one.

Proper selfishness requires that we be ourselves but at the same time remain conscious of others who are also entitled to be properly selfish. The compromises this dilemma requires are only possible if we understand that our own full potential is only realized through living and working with others. St. Augustine,

back in the sixth century, put it well: "In essentials Unity, in
non-essentials Freedom, in all things Charity."

LIVING WITH OTHERS

We may be responsible for ourselves today but we are not as
solitary as some make out. The picture of an atomized society,
trusting no one, confiding in no one, is exaggerated. Most people, over 70 percent in Britain, still live in a household headed by
a married couple. In America that figure is 78 percent, in the
1991 census. The family, it seems, is far from dead. The 1996–7
British Social Attitudes survey showed that only 9 percent of the
population with a living father never see him. Only 3 percent
with a living mother never see her. One third have helped their
parents with regular care in the past five years and only one in
ten disagreed that "people should keep in touch with close family
members even if they don't have much in common." We like, it
seems, to huddle together, as long as we also have our own
space.

If we want somewhere to learn about ourselves, these family
huddles ought to be one of the places we turn to first. Although
they often fail us, they should be the best schools for life. The
reasons are interesting. To learn anything other than the stuff
you find in books, you need to be able to experiment, to make
mistakes, to accept feedback, and to try again. It doesn't matter
whether you are learning to ride a bike or starting a new career,
the cycle of experiment, feedback, and new experiment is always
there. But you won't risk mistakes if you think you will be
punished. You have to be sure of forgiveness if it is a genuine
mistake. You won't accept criticism or negative feedback either,
unless you are sure that it comes from someone whom you

respect, someone who you know has your interests at heart. In jargon it is called "unconditional positive regard."

Parents know about unconditional positive regard, particularly when their children are young. More simply, they call it love. Children are remarkably resilient if they are surrounded by love. If they are not, it can scar them for life, because they have no experience of the emotional safety which love provides. It has been suggested that 70 percent of teenage crime in Britain is committed by young people suffering from "a lack of affection," leading to serious "depression." We should not need technical terms to remind us that a lack of love soon destroys any sense of pride in oneself.

The evidence on the worth of so-called appraisal interviews in organizations is damning. Well-meant occasions, intended to provide helpful feedback on past performance and suggestions for improvement, they almost always end up with the person receiving the appraisal feeling angry and unappreciative. None of us likes to be criticized. The best way to cope with any criticism that comes our way is either to deny that it is justified—"what is your evidence?" we demand indignantly—or to lower our opinion of the critic, so that we don't have to take the criticism seriously. Adopt either of these defensive tactics and any chance of learning is gone. We have also, in the process, rejected the feedback and lost our respect for authority. Most of those institutional appraisal systems end up by damaging morale and changing nothing.

I still find, after all these years, that I need some psychological "stroking" at least once a week, someone to say "that was great" or "you really did an excellent job there." Any critic becomes my enemy, if not for life, then until the next favorable review. Actors want an appreciative audience and at least two curtain calls every night. "How then," I ask managers, "do you think that people in your organizations can survive with one psychological stroke a year, usually combined with some well-intended but critical comment?" Our self-respect is a fragile thing, even if we pretend otherwise—damage it and we cease to listen.

On the other side of the coin, studies of executives in international firms have shown that those who cope best with changing cultures are those who had the most change in their early lives, who were moved around from place to place and school to school, but were always surrounded by love. Given the safety net of love, children can accept anything that comes their way because they do not know that it is unusual. The more exposure to life we can get in our early years, the better, it seems, provided always that there is that unconditional positive regard.

Sadly, not all families provide that positive regard. Some see it as sentimentality. I know one family who can only be complimentary to a stranger. The parents see their role as instructors and correctors of their children, even when they are grown up. Their first comment to a son returning from a three-month trip was, "Look at the state of your clothes!" Not the welcome he had been looking forward to. Other parents regard any behavior that is different from theirs as deviant. To them, learning is imitation of them and their ways. Some families do not like each other, or do not care. Children of such families may need to escape in order to grow. Sadly they will not have learned the necessity of others if they are to be fully themselves. They may have been cheated of a life.

Schools, as the official institutions of learning, ought to be better. Not all are. Only one of my teachers felt any positive regard for me, and that wasn't unconditional. But without the security of positive regard, we can become defensive in explaining ourselves, guarded and private. Our path to any proper understanding of our potential is then blocked. Life can seem to be no more than a treadmill, a long trudge without meaning. Self-ishness then becomes self-indulgence, a way of relieving the tedium, of making the most of an uninviting prospect.

I have changed my career four times now, departing each time of my own accord, or, as some would say, before I was pushed. Each time it was a step into the unknown, and each time I was sacrificing some financial security for a new experience. With hindsight it was always the right thing to do, because it exposed another aspect of myself. But at the time the risks always seemed greater than the rewards. It was my wife who put the risks into perspective, seeing better than I could what was likely to be right for us. Because I knew that she had that positive regard for me, I listened.

Not everyone is so lucky. Families, however they are made up, still matter hugely. People still hanker after permanent partnerships; love is still at the heart of the matter. To be loved, to be held in genuine affection, is the best foundation for learning about oneself. Such love does not have to be uncritical, nor undemanding. In fact, the more demanding and the more exacting in its expectations the better for our learning, provided that the love is synonymous with unconditional positive regard. John Stuart Mill may have been a little optimistic when he described the family as a school of sympathy, tenderness, and loving forgetfulness of self, but families are still the best springboards for life that we have.

Love matters—but, conversely, so does the giving of love, and the responsibility that involves. I have suggested earlier that self-respect comes from responsibility, so that, in another paradox, we are only in a fit state to take responsibility for ourselves when we have learned to take responsibility for others. That, maybe, is why families are so important, not just for the children, but for the parents.

I remember my emotions when I looked at our first-born child, minutes after she had been born—a strange mixture of amazement that she should be so complete, and, at the same time, an awesome awareness of what this entailed; we two inexperienced young people were now responsible for this new life which we had created, and would continue to be so for a good twenty years, or until she would be free to embark on her own pursuit of the white stone. She changed our lives, not just in the logistic details, but in the way we thought about our lives and the future. I think that we grew up overnight.

We have all, no doubt, at times toyed with the idea of love without responsibility, the kind of love we see so often on movie screens or in books. Such meetings of two hearts may be fun for a while, but they dissolve if the fun runs out for either partner. They don't provide the basis for any serious exploration of life's possibilities, because the responsibility for the other's life is not there. This is love as leisure, not love as life. The two are very different. For our own sakes, we need to distinguish between the two, lest we make commitments that we cannot deliver.

The biggest obstacle to proper selfishness in society may be a lack of proper love, and of the responsibility that goes with it. An adolescence that is prolonged until the mid or late thirties, as is now almost the norm, is an excuse to treat love as leisure, to avoid responsibility for anyone or anything, and so to postpone the start of our search for our real identity and for some purpose in our life.

Responsibility, of course, does not come only from love. Work almost always brings a responsibility for others, whether it be for the child you teach, the patient in your care, the work group or the customer, the job to be finished or the project organized. My first real job, as manager of a marketing company in Borneo, in charge of some 120 people, with no telephone line back to the head office in Singapore, was a big step in growing up, in my developing self-respect. I was, in truth, rather frightened. My boss, when sending me there, had regretted that because it was an emergency replacement, there had been no time for training. "So," he said, "I think that we had best go down to the cathedral and say a little prayer!" We didn't, but I got the point. I was on my own, and, in the end, proud of the responsibility.

How awful, then, must it be to have neither love nor work. That this should be the case for so many is the real shame of our modern societies. Given that the ILO has announced that their surveys showed that one third of all workers in the world were currently unemployed or under-employed, proper selfishness requires that we try to do something about it, unless we are happy to live in the middle of a society of human discards. This is a key issue which will be tackled, as far as it can be tackled, in the third part of this book.

WORKING WITH OTHERS

Visions of a world of telecommuters, eyes locked to their screens, marooned in their homes or their work cabins, seeing no one, meeting no one, have always been much exaggerated. If it's too lonely, it's ineffective. In John Naisbitt's words, Hi-Tech will always need to be balanced by Hi-Touch. I have myself suggested that portfolio work is the way of the future for many of us, particularly later in life, but the self-employed will be unlikely to exceed 20 percent of the workforce (they are now 13 percent in Britain) in the foreseeable future, and even when you are categorized as self-employed, you are seldom on your own. You are working with or for someone else on their problems. If you aren't, you are on your way to bankruptcy.

Organizations are being dismantled, but they are then being reassembled in a different way. A blend of skills and personalities is still needed to get most jobs done. Businesses today resemble the sign posted at a building site, listing the huge array of subcontracted firms and individuals involved in the project. But that array still has to be managed, and, as organizations are finding, it may be cheaper but it is much more difficult to manage people when they aren't your people. Ironically, the more independent and autonomous we get, the more we have to learn to work with others. Much of the time, however, we have to work with people we do not see or meet, except occasionally.

Trust is at the heart of it. That seems obvious and trite, yet most of our institutions tend to be arranged on the assumption that people cannot be trusted or relied upon, even in tiny matters. The systems are set up to prevent anyone doing the wrong thing, whether by accident or design. The courier could not find our remote cottage the other day. He called his base on his radio link and they called us, to ask directions. He was just around the corner but in the chain of communications a vital part of the directions got left out. He called them again, and they called us. Once more it happened, this time to ask whether we had a dangerous dog or not. When he and his van eventually arrived we asked whether it would not have been simpler and less aggravating to everyone if he had called us directly from the roadside telephone booth where he had been parked. "We can't do that," he said, "because they won't refund any money we spend."

"But it's only pennies," we exclaimed.

"I know," he said, "but that only shows how little they trust us!"

Writ large, that sort of attitude means a paraphernalia of systems, checkers, and checkers checking checkers—expensive, and deadening. Some commentators have argued that what they call the "audit mania," or the need for some independent inspection, is a virus infecting our society. It is happening, they suggest, because we no longer trust people to act on behalf of anything except their own short-term interests. This, too quickly, becomes a self-fulfilling prophecy. "If they don't trust me, why should I bother to put their needs before mine?" Responsibility then becomes unnecessary, and where there is no responsibility there is no sense of pride, of ownership, of self-respect. But, on the other hand, without some commitment from the individual, trust will not be offered. To be good at your job, or even renowned in your field, will not, in itself, be enough, because we all have to work with others, one way or another, and that requires a degree of mutual trust.

My Oxford college was noted mainly, people used to say, for its ability to go backwards faster than all the others. They were referring to its skill on the river, and that odd phenomenon, at which its team excelled, of eight people going backwards as fast as they can without speaking to each other, steered by the one person who can't row—a typical example of an English team, I would joke, and a demonstration of the English class system at work, the incompetent in charge of the competent. I stopped joking after one Olympic oarsman pointed out that it was the perfect example of a team, for how could they go backwards so fast without communicating, *unless* they had great confidence in each other's skill, trusted everyone to do his best, knew what their goal was, and were totally committed to reaching it, whatever the inconveniences or personal sacrifices?

It was intriguing, therefore, to see the same message emerging from a 1996 film, *True Blue*, which was even filmed in the selfsame college. The film would seem too corny to be true, except that it was. After Oxford's defeat by Cambridge in the annual boat race, some star-studded American rowing champions were drafted in for the next year's race, as temporary students at the university. They try to take over the running of the boat and the preparations for the race, effectively mutiny, are outfaced and dropped from the crew. With only twenty-five days remaining the coach has to train a new crew against all the odds, but he builds a team and they win the race.

"Eagles don't flock" was one of Ross Perot's trademark phrases in the last two American presidential campaigns, arguing that it was a gutsy individualism that made a nation great. It's a theme that is hammered out in *True Blue,* with the Americans and their supporters convinced that the eight best individuals will make the best team, and that it won't matter that every one of those individuals is, if he's honest, doing it for his own sake and to boost his own career. In the end, however, as all managers know well, a good team is more than the sum of its individuals, and prima donnas can sometimes do more harm than good to the common cause.

Yet it is prima donnas whom we seem to want these days. One effect of the rise of the professional, I have argued, is that the best individuals now have access to a global marketplace, giving the elite few a choice of rewards far in excess of those available to people who are almost but not quite as good. The very best lawyers, the cream of the traders, even the best managers, are now like sports stars, wanted everywhere, at any price. Asked how one member of a finance house could possibly be worth the $10 million bonus that he was awarded one year, the chief executive explained that he had earned the firm $60 million in extra profits. If his work had not been so highly rewarded, the argument went, that individual would have gone elsewhere in due course. What does loyalty mean when the stakes are now so high?

Building a flock with these sorts of high-priced eagles around is not going to be easy, but in life, as in a boat, one star does not make a great crew, unless that star is prepared to commit himself or herself to the common cause. The complicated rearrangements of the order of rowing in the boat, which are made much of in the final part of *True Blue,* are a demonstration that individuals have to be prepared to sacrifice their preferences and their pride if the team is to win. For that to happen the cause has to matter. Where that cause is missing or mundane, the temptation to maximize personal ambitions or personal gain is understandable and often irresisitible.

Ross Perot is wrong. Untrammelled individualism corrupts a nation. It leads to an emphasis on rights, with no regard to duties or responsibilities. It breeds distrust and jealousy—and lots of lawyers. If we can leave families when we feel like it, are free to ignore or insult our neighbors, treat organizations as stepping stones on a personal trip, and only make friends with people who will be useful contacts, to be discarded when no longer needed, we will erode that "social capital" which more and more people are recognizing as the bedrock of a successful and prosperous society.

Bribery won't win the lasting loyalty of the rich eagles, or make them ready to sacrifice. They can always get more elsewhere. "All our best workers are volunteers," says Microsoft, meaning that, being already millionaires several times, there is no financial need for them to work. The excitement and the challenge of the work are what keep them there. We do not have to emulate either the rewards or the workaholism of Microsoft, but we can still accept the challenge of asking, "Would they work here if they didn't need to?" It is a question that even the old vocations of medicine and teaching are having to ask as we all become more mercenary. Unfortunately the answer is not going to be as easy as the challenge of winning a boat race.

The eagles, too, have to ask themselves whether the prizes are really worth the loneliness of the high flyer. If friends are only contacts, they can drop you in their turn, when you are no longer useful. To those who make no commitment, no commitment is on offer when it is needed. A champion's life is often short, and trophies are no substitute in the end for a shared commitment to something beyond oneself.

CONNECTED TO OTHERS

Francis Fukuyama, in his important book on trust, takes the matter of trust beyond the boundaries of the organization. The prosperity of societies depends, he says, on relationships of trust, which reach beyond the family or the organization. Familial societies such as Italy or China today find it hard to put their confidence in anyone outside the family. They cannot therefore build large organizations, because these inevitably involve outsiders. Fukuyama believes that this will prevent these countries creating truly global organizations. Maybe they do not want or need to.

On the other hand, individualist countries, such as the Anglo-Saxon societies of America and Britain, can become very legalistic places, unwilling to believe that the hospital did its best or that the other driver was not at fault. Such a lack of trust in others can become very expensive, because neither the law nor insurance comes cheap.

De Tocqueville, looking at America a century and a half ago, was worried about individualism which, he said, "at first, only saps the virtues of public life, but in the long run . . . attacks and destroys all others and is at length absorbed in downright selfishness." He believed that the network of civil associations (clubs, churches, schools, political parties, community groups,

sports clubs, etc.) played an important part in combating individualism and limiting its potentially destructive consequences.
This is the "social capital" that writers like Robert Putnam in
America are worried may be eroding. In my terms, selfishness is
no longer "proper" in a society which has allowed individualism
to become so isolating.

America grew rich because its individualism was tempered by
a willingness to trust or rely upon outsiders who held the same
values and beliefs. Thus there was this paradox in America of a
very individualist ethic combined with a conformist society. A
good paradox, one might say, but confusing when you first meet
it—all these individuals trumpeting their individuality but wearing exactly the same clothes and eating the same food. America
was, and is, a society which prefers to put its trust in civil associations rather than government, a society which has defined
rights but accepts some civic responsibilities as the norm. More
than any other country, local officialdom is elected locally, and
religion, with its codes of behavior, plays a larger part in American life than in most other Western countries. Trust, in the sense
of confidence in the community, was once high, and probably
still is, although there are signs, now, of a retreat into their very
different ghettoes by the rich and poor alike, with their differing
value systems going with them.

Apart from our kith and kin, we soon establish other sorts of
families: networks and professional associations, or "hives," for
the knowledge workers; clubs for the enthusiasts and teams for
the sportive; committees and campaigns for the civic-minded.
These "communities of interest," some of them now meeting in
cyberspace rather than the clubroom, are the new kinds of
neighborhoods, more important in the lives of many than the
physical neighborhoods where they live. People need people, and
they find them, most of the time. It is these communities that

give real expression to our concern for others, to our need to belong to something wider than our own little nest. In all of them trust is balanced against commitment. Where there is no commitment there can be no trust.

It is fashionable both to speak in favor of "community," "partnership," and "responsible citizenship" as the link pieces of an individualist society, and at the same time to lament the demise of our traditional communities. A recent report on the changes to Swindon, one of Britain's old industrial towns turned into a new-style hub for the technological and information businesses of today, should give us hope.

Swindon is not a place to lift the heart at first sight. The place was once known for the workshops that built trains and carriages for the railways of the steam age, a very utilitarian place. It has, the report says, no focus, no cathedral, no university, no beauty. Its citizens are mainly technological sophisticates but they have suffered from labor mobility, de-industrialization, and delayering in the organizations. Nevertheless, the report was optimistic in its conclusion. "The town's capacity for civic regeneration has proved considerable. Its citizens . . . have achieved quietly successful race relations; they participate in an ever-widening range of voluntary groups; their churches are diversifying the services they offer, and their schools are expanding their role as civic institutions. In ways mundane and intriguing, the people of Swindon are learning to live with the hectic forces of modernity which one of them described as "the vagabond way." In their unhistoric acts there are lessons for us all." For Swindon read Pittsburgh, one more example of an out-of-date city reborn by the energy of its citizens and their commitment in a different future. Communities can recreate themselves if they want to enough.

The latticework of "families" is one way in which society

bonds together. As important is the set of codes by which people behave and relate to each other. These are the accepted rules and values without which any society disintegrates because there is no restraint on individualism. In their absence the world does indeed become a jungle where only the most improperly selfish survive. These codes are caught, however, not taught. They are caught from the examples that we find in the different "families" we meet over time.

The genetic family is the first of these, soon augmented by the school and, perhaps more crucially, by the peer group of our schoolmates. These early groups establish the framework through which we view the world. Their importance cannot be exaggerated, because young children accept whatever they are given as the way the world is. As they grow older they need more models to choose from. They should, therefore, be exposed to as many different groups and associations as is possible. Until I left college I had not met any adults other than my parents and their friends, or my teachers. Cosy universe though it was, in my case, it was also a partial world. Other worlds are not so cosy or so decent, yet they set the rules and the codes for the young who grow up in them.

An American study, *Beyond the Classroom* by Laurence Steinberg, which looked at the academic results of twenty thousand high school students, came up with convincing evidence that Asian children did better than other groups, not because of any genetic differences, nor because of better parenting, but because of the norms and values of the peer group. Black students, according to Steinberg, do not really believe that doing poorly in school will hurt their chances of success afterwards. Asian students have a greater fear of the consequences of failure and this provides a strong motivation to work hard at school. "Something in Asian students' lives protects them, even if they are exposed to less-than-perfect parenting," concludes Steinberg, "while something in black students' lives undermines the positive effects of parental involvement."

Communities or "families" of different sorts are, therefore, the moral reinforcing rods of society. When they fail, the law has to fill the gap, but laws are clumsy instruments, expensive and always applied after the event. We need to be connected to others more informally in order to learn the rules of life. It is always possible, of course, that we find "families" whose codes may be antithetical to a good society, a mafia of one variety or another. That has always been one of the unwanted outcomes of prison— the introduction to a new criminal "family," with its own codes. To this there is no answer except to find more appropriate "families" to provide examples of other codes. For this reason community service of one sort or another is championed by many as a better alternative than prison. It won't, however, prove to be better unless the service is built around groups or "families" which will offer not only work and a disciplined structure but also some unconditional support, forgiveness for genuine mistakes, and a tolerance of differences.

In time we learn to build our own "families" with their own rules and support mechanisms. Life would be empty without them. One friend wrote recently of her field in Wales. She grows trees there, trees given to her in memory of loved ones. It is a field for others. She also wrote of her long correspondence with one Leroy Simmonds who was, she said, on death row in Jamaica when they first started corresponding. Now, she said with some pride, he is in the general penitentiary and she is still working with Amnesty International and the United Nations to get him released. I don't think that she has ever met him, but by taking some responsibility for his life she has given him the kind of unconditional support he needs and has been able to live out more of her personal dream.

Cousin Mollie was ninety-five when she died. For the previous ten years she had lain in bed, weak but not ill. She had never married and had no close family. She saw only her paid caretakers, about whom she regularly complained. Life, on the surface, had no meaning for her. Yet her funeral was attended by sixty people of all ages, many from distant parts of the country. It turned out that she was a great letter writer and had maintained a steady correspondence with a wide range of people over the years. She had created her own family. Her life was not the empty shell it seemed.

Towards a Decent Society

The ideas in the second part of this book apply to the institutions of society as much as they do to individuals. Capitalism needs to be reinterpreted to make it decent, and companies, which are the key institutions of capitalism, need to be rethought. Education should be redesigned to prepare us all for more personal responsibility. Government needs to return responsibility to the people. Only then can we feel that life and society is ours to shape. Were that to happen our values could dictate the way things worked, rather than the other way round.

EIGHT

A Better Capitalism

L EFT TO themselves, things do not necessarily work out for the best. Laissez-faire is value free. No one is responsible for anyone else. That is improper selfishness and can self-destruct. We need something better. Capitalism as an idea includes social capital as well as economic capitalism. One without the other will not work for long.

A decent capitalism will be built on enterprises that are properly selfish. They will be properly concerned with survival and achievement but will strive to be inner directed, to express their personalities and their beliefs in what they do. They are not just the instruments of their owners. They will be companies who aim for immortality and hope that they will deserve it, companies who are communities not properties, who see their people as citizens with all that that implies, and who understand that they need an implicit license to operate in their societies, where they are citizens too. These changes require a change in attitude more

than a change in law. We can make it happen ourselves, if we are
so determined.

THE PRIVILEGE OF IMMORTALITY

Business is wont to say that its purpose is to create profit and
improve the bottom line, or, more grandiosely, to increase shareholder value. Profit is essential for survival, and survival, I have
argued earlier, is the first of the three steps to fulfillment, for
business as well as individuals. But to make survival your priority
still begs the question, Mahler's question, survival for what? If a
business cannot answer that question, it will seem, to outsiders,
to be interested only in itself. Its owners and managers will regard it as their instrument, having no personality or purpose of
its own.

In recent years business has been under pressure to increase
its efficiency. The easiest way to do this is to reduce numbers, of
both people and pay. The downsizing, outsourcing, and reduction in benefits which followed could only emphasize the idea of
the employees as the instruments of the owners. Shareholders
come first, was the message of the new streamlined business,
customers an essential second, and the people who do the work
a necessary third. No wonder business began to seem inhuman,
yet one more scherzo for the fortunate. I have used the past
tense because there are some hints of change.

The shareholders, however, have to be behind the idea of the
company as a person in its own right. As it is, in the Anglo-Saxon
countries, a large chunk of those shareholders are the pension
funds. Their principal interest is in a constant stream of dividends which will allow them the cash to pay out the pensions.
They want a cash cow. Not for them is there the choice of

forgoing today's cash for tomorrow's growth. As a result British and American businesses pay out dividends far higher than their Japanese or continental European competitors.

I remember standing on the roof of a factory at the center of a small Belgian town. The chairman of the business, a family firm, explained that the factory was essential to the life of the town below us. "We saw them through two world wars," he said, "and we shall see them through the current recession." Profit was therefore essential, he stressed, but everyone understood the reason. Family businesses where the owners are also the managers, and are competent enough to do the job, understand Mahler's question. Ten years later, that chairman is dead. The family is no longer involved in the management. It is now more interested in dividends than in Mahler's question. When ownership becomes divorced from management, as in all public companies, Mahler's question is easy to ignore.

It is an odd irony that it was the prudent Anglo-Saxon tradition of investing the pension reserves outside the business, instead of keeping them inside, as in Germany and Italy for example, that effectively created the huge stock markets of London and Wall Street and made them such powerful engines of growth. Now that same tradition bleeds businesses of money, money which does not, on the whole, go back into any business but which either gets paid out to pensioners or is used to buy other shares from other shareholders. This secondary market, buying other people's shares, is froth on the surface of enterprise. It is odd, when you think of it, that it should be given so much importance. The problem is that the immediacy of this secondary market can often divert attention from the real purpose and identity of the business.

In truth, the only justifiable purpose of a business is to create and add value, to make something happen that wasn't there before, or, if it was already there, to make it better, or cheaper, or available to more people. How that added value is distributed and to whom is another matter. When a business ceases to add value it dies, killed by the market which it has failed to satisfy. That is the principle justification for the market—it roots out the inefficient and rewards the successful. A successful business is, therefore, one that continues to add value—forever.

Life everlasting, then? Strangely it is not impossible. Businesses and other organizations have a privilege denied to ordinary mortals—they don't have to die. They can live beyond our graves, and can truly aim for indefinite, if not everlasting, life. The Mitsui corporation and my Oxford College are both more than six hundred years old and still going strong. The Catholic Church is older still. When the Royal Dutch Shell Group looked around for some contemporaries as it reached its centenary it found thirty companies, varying in age from one hundred to seven hundred years old, scattered throughout Europe, Japan, and North America, with names such as Siemens and DuPont. The Swedish company Sora survived the Middle Ages, the Reformation, the wars of the 1600s, the Industrial Revolution, and two world wars.

To live that long, however, you have to deserve it. Most don't, and quite properly die or get absorbed into something bigger and better. Because to live that long you have to know not only what you stand for, to be sure of your central values and your reason for existing, but you also have to change constantly what you do and how you do it, to grow better although not necessarily bigger, and to have a continuing passion for your work—all exactly as documented by the research into long-lasting companies. Arie de Geus of Shell describes these companies as river companies, always flowing, unlike the puddle companies which evaporate in the heat. The Catholic Church is currently under pressure to change some of its rules but not its central values. The question then arises: which rules are really central values? The wrong answer to this question has proved disastrous to organizations in the past.

THE CORPORATE WHITE STONE

Americans are increasingly talking about the "soul" and the personality of an organization. By soul they mean the spirit and the atmosphere that pervade the workplace, something that is more than the structure or the systems or even than the financial rewards. Cynics might mock and claim that George III's chancellor, Baron Thurlow, was right when he said, two hundred years ago, "How can you expect a corporation to have a conscience, when it has no soul to be damned and no body to be kicked?" Times move on, however, and the argument of this chapter is that unless organizations have both a soul and a conscience they will not deserve their place in modern society and will not long survive. Organizations, in other words, also need to find their own white stone, to know what their *telos* or consuming purpose is, for they, too, are hungry spirits at heart, searching for the meaning in all their striving.

Dean Berry, an American consultant and writer, says, "If we are to feel spiritually rewarded, we cannot allow our lives to continue to be compartmentalized, divided or labelled." The new workers want to bring their whole personalities to work with them, they want to feel at ease and at one with the aims and values of the organization. An observer of Netscape, the Internet software company, said, "The only people who work this hard are people who want to. The only people who want to are people with enough freedom to do the things they want to do. Netscape is a company that consciously undermanages." Echoes there of Microsoft's "volunteers." Both of these companies are held together by the spirit of the place. Lose that spirit and I suspect that the business will collapse, because the people will leave. "Spirit," "soul," "personality"—these words crop up too often to be ignored. Language is often the herald of change.

The successful company will try to ensure that its soul and its personality or essence outlive the transient careers of its people. It must aim for immortality, even though it may never achieve it. The average life of the Fortune 500 businesses is only forty years. How dared they, one wonders, have the arrogance, not so long ago, to offer fifty-year careers?

"Soul" is one of those concepts that, like beauty, evaporates when you try to define it, but like beauty it is instantly recognizable when you meet it. Organizations have a feel about them, a feel which the visitor picks up as soon as he or she enters the building or, often, merely encounters one of the people who work there. There is an abundance of what can best be called the "E" factors, when "E" stands for energy, enthusiasm, effort, excitement, excellence, and so on. More than that, the talk is about "we," not "I," and there is a sense that the organization is on some sort of crusade, not just to make money, but something grander, something worthy of one's commitment, skills, and time.

A match of corporate and individual souls releases those "E" factors. Without that match, work and life are dull. David Whyte puts it well in one of his poems:

Always this energy smoulders inside;
when it remains unlit
the body fills with dense smoke.

An organization that leaves the individual souls imprisoned and unlit fills itself with smoke. It is not only inefficient, it is indecent. We need the chance, in our work, not just in our leisure, to discover some of the truth about ourselves. If the findings about the motivations of the young of today are correct—that they want money, yes, but after that the chance to use their brains and to control their own time, to have the freedom to express themselves—then any organization that remains a prison for their souls will soon lose the best of its young.

The senior partners of an international consulting firm once came to me with a problem, looking for a neat solution. They recruited some of the best and the brightest in the land, they said, but they were disturbed by how many of them were leaving after two or three years, some of the best ones, too, apparently. "The odd thing is, they are not leaving to join our competitors for more money or more seniority—that we could understand—they are going into strange occupations like teaching or temporary work, or just backpacking around the world for a year or two."

"Do you ask them *why* they are leaving?" I said.

"Oh yes, but they just tend to say that it's not right for them."

I suggested that they had discovered that their own priorities were not in line with the *telos* or goals of the organization and that their driven days then left no room for their self-expression. They were blocked in their search for the white stone.

I could see that it wasn't the advice that the firm wanted, or understood. For the senior partners the essence of their lives was the work they did. That was where their souls found their true nesting place. But the work that suited them might not be right for all. Souls must match if the organization is to live. A senior manager of Oxfam, the British-based charity, says that he receives a constant stream of young people who have left their high-paying jobs in consultancy or finance and come to Oxfam in search of work in which they can believe.

In the search for their soul, or their essence, companies and other organizations come up with "mission statements" or documents headed "Vision and Values." Unsure, sometimes, how to do this, they hire consultants to advise them. I have known world-famous organizations whose mission statements were written for them by so-called strategic consultants. That is rather like asking your psychoanalyst to tell you who you are. Such organizations truly are soulless places, machines with human parts, dedicated to efficiency but not effectiveness.

THE NEW ASSETS

These issues become more urgent with the growth of intangible property, the stuff that does not register on the balance sheet—the brands, the research, the networks, the reputation, the know-how, and the "core competencies" of the place. Chief executives have always talked about the importance of their people, but now it's for real because it's financial.

The relationship between the price paid for new acquisitions and the book value of their assets was measured for 391 large American organizations between 1981 and 1993. The mean price was 4.4 times the book value. The difference was not entirely due to that mysterious thing called goodwill, nor to overeager buyers paying over the odds, but was the best estimate, by those buyers, of the intangible assets lying behind the official balance sheet numbers. In 1997, $100 invested in Microsoft would buy you only $1 of fixed tangible assets.

The fact that we can only determine the value of those intangible assets by subtraction reflects the difficulty of measuring them, not the fact that they don't exist. The OECD estimates that more than half of the wealth of advanced industrial societies is now derived from these sorts of assets and that knowledge workers now account for eight out of ten new jobs. The accounts still class these workers as costs, even though everyone knows that they are the crucial assets of any business. Once again, statistics lag behind reality, confusing us all.

In organizations such as investment banks, advertising agencies, or consultancies, there is almost nothing there except these intangibles. The building is leased along with the computers, the cars are on contract, and the carpets are worn down. If anyone buys the business they are buying a customer list, some product brands, and maybe some research, but, mainly, the hope that the best of the people working there will stay with the new owners for the ride. You can put a price on these things, of course, but you can't own any of them (except perhaps the brands and the research) in any true sense of the word. You can't own hope. Those people assets which you have acquired and thought you owned could vanish overnight. The very concept of property becomes unrealistic in this scenario.

It is no longer sensible, perhaps not even moral, for the financiers to claim that they can "own" the skills or the experience of the people in the business. This sort of intangible property can only belong to the individuals who have those skills and that experience. The idea of a community being a piece of property is, in any case, a rather Anglo-Saxon idea, which stems from the early beginnings of capitalism in the seventeenth century, when a business was a ship or a building, a real piece of property. In other countries, such as Japan or Germany, the people in charge understand that they have to share their powers with other interests. How, they ask, can you own something that does not belong to you, will probably outlive you, and is not yours to dispose of?

A Scottish friend of mine, the last in a long line of lairds, was driving an African friend back from the airport to stay with him in his castle. As they drove deep into the highlands, my friend waved his hand expansively at the heather-covered hills all around them—"Now," he said, "you are on my territory, all that you can see belongs to me."

He wasn't boasting, just explaining, but the African was puzzled. "I don't understand," he said. "How can you own a mountain? That belongs to the earth, and to those who live on the earth, and will live on it. Perhaps you mean that you are looking after it for a while, a sort of trustee, maybe?"

"If you put it like that, yes, I suppose so."

My friend told me this story a year later. He said that it had made him realize how we let our language shape the way we think. Of course, he said, ownership was the wrong word, because ownership implies that you have the right to get rid of it if you don't like it, destroy it even. Which is why the idea that a man could own a wife did not survive into modern times, even if some men still act as if it did. It may well be that the idea of the ownership of companies will also not make it far into the next millennium, even if some continue to act as if it still made sense.

If a business is now, in its essentials, a collection of people, it will make more sense to think of it as a town or a village rather than a piece of machinery. This will eventually change the way we think about businesses. It is already changing the way we talk about them. The language of political theory—leadership, constituencies, alliances, power, and influence—is replacing the old engineering and property language of structure, planning, and control, and even management. Talented individuals don't like to be "human resources," or to be managed. They prefer to be led by someone they respect. Try calling a pop star or a leading actor a "resource" and wait for the response—it won't be polite.

Much attention has been paid to the difficult challenge of measuring these new kinds of assets. They have always existed, of course, but never in such predominance. Much too has been said and written about the management of such assets. But not enough has been said about the underlying contracts with the different stakeholders, contracts which now have to change. The shareholders, the so-called owners, must now see themselves more properly as investors. Twenty years ago, in Britain, it was another group of stakeholders who wielded too much power in industry. That group was the unions. They used their power to protect their own short-term interests without too much concern for the life and continuity of the business as a whole. Margaret Thatcher's great contribution was to rein back that power, when her government took over an impoverished and downcast Britain. Today, in Britain, the unions take a more far-sighted view of business, realizing that their interests are ultimately and intimately entwined with those of business as a whole.

It is now the turn of the shareholders, in both Britain and America. Their influence has, in the eyes of many, become too dominant and too separate from the long-term interests of the business. Their role will have to change, preferably with their agreement. Shareholders or their agents will still have a voice, but not for long, I predict, will they be able to use that voice to command or insist on what they want, because the human assets themselves will increasingly demand their own voice. Wise investors will give those assets a say in the control of the business rather than see them leave. The investors may have reduced power in the new arrangement, but they will still have influence, and it is right that they should, because a business run by itself for itself can become lazy and blinkered.

German businesses have long been controlled and directed internally by their own people, including representatives of the unions, with finance and oversight provided by a comfortable cluster of big banks, who are content to wait for the long-term future, reluctant to disturb the status quo in case the new is worse than the familiar. A few near-disasters have made them begin to realize that they need not only the money of outside investors but also the harsher discipline that this interest group will bring. Ten years ago, I heard the then chairman of Daimler-Benz insist that the company would never be listed on the New York Stock Exchange (where no German company at that time appeared) because the perspectives of those investors would distort their priorities.

Five years later the company was listed on that exchange, the first German company to do so. They may well have wished that it had happened earlier, because, prodded by their new share-holders, they might not then have sailed on so complacently into the uncharted waters, for them, of aerospace or waited so long to move any of their manufacturing out of expensive Germany, or to develop smaller and cheaper cars for a less expensive market-place. I would be surprised, however, if the outside investors were ever allowed to be numerous enough to sell the company. Investors they may be, with a voice to be listened to and share prices to influence; owners they are not.

The psychological contract with the new knowledge workers is another issue. It could be seen as a purely commercial transac-tion—money for skills and time, and more money for better re-sults, and forget all the niceties. Bribery in return for loyalty, in other words, on the principle that we are all mercenaries, on hire to the highest bidder, but in a winner-take-all world where the best can command so much more than the next best, this can be a very expensive option. Mercenaries owe loyalty only to them-selves, with a temporary commitment to their current project and no commitment beyond that to the organization. This is a

poor basis for immortality, since the mercenaries will be unpre-
pared to trade short-term benefits for longer-term growth. Why
should I do what I don't want to do, or go where I don't want to
go, just for the good of the organization?

Organizations will need to distinguish between mercenaries
and citizens. Mercenaries are those hired for their specialist
skills, to be dispensed with when no longer needed. The contract
is clear, even if we dress it up as employability, which is corpo-
rate-speak for "it's really up to you, don't count on us." Citizens
are different: they are full members of the organizational state,
enjoying a reciprocal commitment. Citizens traditionally enjoy,
at the very least, a right of residence, access to justice, freedom
of speech, a share in the wealth of society, and a say in its
governance, through elections or referenda. In return they implicitly or, in some countries, explicitly, promise to obey the laws
and to be loyal to the state. The implications of a corporate
citizenry will be explored in the next chapter.

THE CORPORATION AS A CITIZEN

Corporations not only have citizens, they *are* citizens. They have
rights in the societies where they operate, but they also have
responsibilities which law and custom impose on them. We increasingly expect our corporate citizens to act decently. At the
very least they need an informal license to operate, as the Tomorrow's Company Inquiry at the Royal Society of Arts in London
described it.

Some would argue that behaving decently is justifiable because it is, in the long run, good for the bottom line. A company
that is mean, spiteful, and ungenerous to its surrounding communities will only have fair-weather friends. Therefore, an in-

vestment beyond the call of duty which builds friends for hard times is a good investment. Grand Metropolitan, the London-based food and drinks multinational, which spends $20 million annually on community involvement, believes that it creates a virtuous circle and has produced an input/output matrix to demonstrate this. Others see it as self-evident. As Roberto Guizueta of Coca-Cola put it: "While we were once perceived as simply providing services, selling products and employing people, business now shares in much of the responsibility for our global quality of life. Successful companies will handle this heightened sense of responsibility quite naturally, if not always immediately. I say this not because successful business leaders are altruistic at heart. I can assure you many are not. I say it because they will demand that their companies will remain intensely focused on the needs of their customers and consumers."

Others ask whether altruism is not possible, whether it is not enough to behave well for the sake of behaving well. Does generosity and a care for those around you have to be justified by anything other than a generous spirit? A care for all those who have a stake in the business, be they served by it or serving it, is seen by some as the proper duty of every business. John Kay and John Plender, two advocates of a British version of stakeholding as the model for businesses, speak of stakeholding as responsible individualism. Responsible individualism is another name for proper selfishness.

In the past, rich individuals were the patrons of the arts, enriching their communities by their choice of architects, sculptors, and artists; they financed charities, established foundations, and endowed museums and art galleries. Whether it was genuine benevolence that inspired them, a stake in immortality, or vainglorious pride, they were judged to be worthy citizens. Today, as much is expected of the corporate citizen if they, too, are to be judged worthy. I am hopeful that the halls and forecourts of our businesses may yet come to resemble the churches of Tuscany, as exhibition spaces for our artists, open to all who might pass by. It is encouraging, also, to see the names of big and small firms on the programs of new opera companies, local theaters, and city music festivals. Guilty industrialists and bankers financed the Renaissance, and we are forever in their debt. Those who make economic capital would be wise to create some accompanying social capital or they will erode the society which surrounds them.

In Britain, as in America, many major companies have taken the point and have recognized the importance of investing in their surrounding communities, either directly or through intermediate agencies. The businesses bring their skills and their physical facilities to schools, deprived communities, and young entrepreneurs, and contribute to the improvement of the environment. These initiatives have introduced many business leaders and young executives to areas where they had seldom trod before. The process does not only help the communities, it can wonderfully expand the horizons and the experience of the executives and their companies. It is too easy to get lost in one's own busyness and to assume that others have your priorities.

A recent survey, however, made it clear that the general public in Britain still expects much more community involvement from business. The license to operate is still waiting to be validated. Gestures alone are not enough to qualify one as a genuine citizen. The charitable suggestion would be that the public is uninformed. There are more good citizens than they realize. More facts and numbers would therefore help. The London Benchmarking Group consists of six major UK companies who are trying to put some hard facts into the reporting of their community activities so that they are more transparent and their impact more easily assessed. Six companies don't make a mountain, but their example may encourage others. As GrandMet says: "Businesses can make major contributions to societies over and above the satisfaction of customer and shareholder needs." The more those contributions are made visible, the more easily will people believe that capitalism can be decent.

Businesses in Britain have discovered social entrepreneurs: the growing number of energetic individuals who take it upon themselves to make something happen in their local environment, be it a new arts center, a hospice or housing association, a scheme for re-engaging young people in the workforce or for educating children out of school. Businesses have more of an affinity with entrepreneurs than with local councils or large not-for-profit bureaucracies. Businesses are happier to lend their resources to such people because they have more confidence that they will be properly used. They may even hope to find models in the behavior of these social entrepreneurs that could be useful to them in their own business. Altruism is not to be sniffed at just because it helps you as well as others.

Maybe we should look elsewhere for our models. Charles Hampden-Turner tells the story of Intel in Penang, Malaysia, where the Pentium processor is made. "The managing director, a Chinese Malaysian, described how he had started an in-house shop. Why? 'To save time,' he explained, 'but also to generate profits, which we used to start the credit union. Now we have taken capital in the credit union and invested it in low- and medium-tech corporations in this area . . . it is so that any employee who has worked for us loyally but cannot learn the trigonometry needed for Pentium production can be outplaced in a company which our union partly owns. We find jobs for everyone.'

"We were standing in the middle of a flower garden which was also the day nursery. The children were learning English: 'Good morning, visitor!' they chorused. Managers' children are educated at cost, technicians' at half-cost, workers' children are educated free." Economic capital and social capital go well together.

It is because the corporate citizen can be a force for good where other agents can't that the concept of corporate citizenship is so important. Christian Aid is spearheading a campaign in Britain, called Change the Rules, to prod the big supermarket chains into using their purchasing power to improve working conditions in third world countries. Christian Aid claims that children aged six are working on coffee plantations in Brazil and that the demand for good quality grapes had produced a reliance on pesticides which damage workers' health. To sell or consume food produced in this way is, they say, exploitation, and the signs are that more and more people are agreeing with them. Christian Aid has persuaded two food chains to start work on a pilot project to improve working conditions in several developing countries. The top ten chains have an annual turnover equal to the income of the world's poorest thirty-five countries and therefore can, says the charity, afford the changes. Oxfam, too, is working with five British retailers to improve conditions for garment workers in the developing world.

"Goods produced under conditions which do not meet a rudimentary standard of decency should be regarded as contraband and ought not to be allowed to pollute channels of interstate trade." That was President Roosevelt speaking, half a century ago. His comment was overwhelmed by the consumers' careless splurge, but consumers now care more. Increasingly, given the choice now available, consumers want to feel empathy towards the companies they buy from, as well as the products that they buy. As companies like Body Shop have shown, enlightened policies bring in enlightened customers, but it works the other way around too—as customers become more enlightened they expect businesses to act as enlightened citizens also.

A refinery in Australia was concerned by the high level of absenteeism among its workforce. Asked at this time to contribute to a fund for the improvement of the local community, the management agreed but added an inspired codicil. For every day of absenteeism they would subtract a percentage from their donation. This condition was announced to all their workers. Within months the absenteeism had fallen to record low levels. Individuals care, it seems, and companies should care also, if they are to represent the concerns of their members.

The customers are having an effect both by their purchasing decisions, their lawsuits, and their campaigning groups. The big companies are changing their ways and their attitudes. The precedent-setting decision forced on the tobacco companies to help fund the health care of those who were harmed by their products would have been unthinkable a few years ago. Responding to vociferous complaints over its actions in the North Sea and Nigeria, Shell International has been publicly candid about its relative insensitivity to environmental issues and has promised to reform. In a speech in California in 1997 the chief executive of another oil company—BP—accepted that his industry had a responsibility to develop alternative forms of energy which were less polluting and promised that his company would lead the way. "The cultures of politics, science, and enterprise," he said, "must work together if we are to match and master the challenges we all face. We share a common vital interest in finding the answers."

THE NEW SOCIAL CONTRACT

Translating the idea of the company as a village and a community into the reality of modern corporate structure is complicated. Most executives are happy to leave the idea on the shelf as an interesting metaphor. This will not be enough in the long run. The soul of a business must be expressed in its constitution, and, if it is going to be more than the instrument of its financiers, who call themselves its owners, the articles of association must reflect the new reality. Examples thus far are few. They include the John Lewis Partnership in Britain. Two less well known cases are given below. More are cited in the next chapter, which is concerned with the management of the new kind of citizen organization.

THE CAMELLIA PHILOSOPHY

Camellia Plc is an unusual company. It is primarily devoted to long-term tree agriculture, with large numbers of tea estates on the Indian subcontinent and in East Africa. To these must be added a wide range of other commercial and industrial interests. It is a publicly quoted company but a majority of the shares are owned by a foundation. The first duty of the foundation is to ensure, through its share control, that Camellia continues to exist for at least one hundred years—a reasonable stab at immortality. That part of the dividends accruing to the foundation which exceeds new capital investment requirements is largely reinvested in the countries where the profits are earned, in schools, hospitals, and ventures to improve the lot of the peoples in those lands.

The remarks of its chairman, Gordon Fox, in the 1995 annual report express the philosophy of the company very clearly.

I appear to be something of a lone voice these days . . . in challenging the conventional view that the shareholders "own" the company and, by extension, that they own the assets of the company. I adopt this position not only because most shareholders, whether they are individuals or institutions . . . are essentially punters . . . but because I was taught to believe that with ownership came responsibility, caring, and concern. I therefore find it difficult to accept the conventional concept of ownership when the marketplace applauds and rewards a company's share price and its management upon its announcement of provisions, often representing years of retained earnings, relating to the redundancy of employees. Particularly since recent studies are now demonstrating that many restructurings have led to permanent damage to the company's infrastructure, let alone morale.

Anyone who has contemplated a great work of art or craft cannot help but observe that there is an indefinable point where the creative process has imbued it with a unique quality whereby it has become transformed into something quite spiritual, a holy grail so to speak. In perhaps a distant way this special quality can also come to exist in a company, which enables it to generate high levels of allegiance and general respect. It also appears to generate its own particular energy levels, which leads to creativity, diversity, and growth. Certainly its particular culture becomes something palpable, and I would maintain that this quality is a most valuable asset and worth sustaining not only for the sake of its employees and others whom it directly affects and influences, but for society at large, because such companies underpin the strength and stability of society and set a valuable example for others to follow.

Camellia has grown and prospered over the years because it is pervaded by a sense of allegiance between colleagues, between employees and, above all, loyalty by the company to those it employs. The resultant environment leads naturally to a quality of motivation that far surpasses that of the carrot of share options, encouraging individual greed, and the stick of threatened redundancy.

Camellia's philosophy offers a vision of a benevolent capitalism which benefits all connected to it, without favoring one group excessively. It will not suit everyone because the narrow base of public holding limits its capacity to raise money from the market. Most firms, however, finance their growth from retained earnings or bank borrowings. Again, it is hard for well-established businesses to get from here to there unless they buy back their own stock and place it in a foundation. Few are profitable enough to do this to the necessary extent. Camellia, however, stands out as a possible model for the future.

BERTELSMANN AG

Bertelsmann is a £8.2 billion media conglomerate, headquartered in Germany, with over sixty thousand employees around the world. Founded in 1835, it is now more than 160 years old. In order to safeguard the continuity of the company, the Bertelsmann/Mohn families have passed the majority of their shares to the Bertelsmann Foundation. Currently this foundation owns 68.8 percent of the equity capital, the Mohn family 20.5 percent, and the ZEIT Foundation, based in Hamburg, 10.7 percent. The Bertelsmann Foundation states in its bylaws that it "exclusively and directly pursues purposes relating to the general welfare." In practice it will invest in education and training enterprises relevant to the media world as well as innovative civic projects.

The company has a major profit-sharing scheme under which the greater part of the profits are shared out among the employees of what Reinhard Mohn, the chairman, calls the partnership. The profit-sharing is realized by issuing profit participation certificates which are listed on the stock exchange. By this method the capital remains in the business as equity. The employees are entitled to sell back their certificates; most of them, however, regard them as additional savings for their old age. Over recent years the certificates have paid an interest rate of 15 percent at an average market rate of 200 percent.

Mohn sees this system as a way of guaranteeing the long-term financial security of the workers, but also as a way of increasing their identity with the company.

The company is unusual in that it has a formal written constitution, with many bylaws. The thrust of the constitution is that ownership carries obligations. In the preamble to the constitution the objectives of the company are set out as follows:

1. The company must make the maximum possible contribution to society. All group interests are subordinate to this goal.

2. Self-fulfillment of all persons working in the company must be made possible on the job. The management is responsible for guaranteeing the internal structures necessary for this, as well as for harmonizing conflicting interests.

3. The company must achieve a profit, in order to ensure

its survival and the jobs it provides. Earnings are used for the formation of new capital, payment of dividends, and employee profit-sharing.

4. The company must support the functions of the state by paying taxes.

There is a section in the formal constitution headed "The Company in Society":

We advocate a free, democratic, and social order in society, because we believe that such an order guarantees the highest degree of personal freedom and the best prerequisites for social development. We believe the following to be necessary:

— A free-market system based on the principle of competition, performance, and a broad distribution of private property. It is the task of the state to assure freedom of choice on the part of the consumer and free competition.

— A social system committed to social responsibility, in which the owners of large assets consisting of means of production acknowledge their responsibility as trustees with regard to the general public.

— An organizational structure in business which gives everyone the same opportunity for personal development and assures a fair distribution of wealth, a share of the means of production, concern for social needs, and a balanced relationship between rights and duties.

Many organizations have something similar in their statements of company philosophy. It is rather different when it is spelled out in a formal constitution which is binding on all members of the company. This is corporate citizenship made real.

THE BIG ONES

The examples cited started life as private firms. Their constitutions were the gift of their founders. The problem is different for the large, publicly owned companies, where it is really an issue of a new type of governance.

Consider these facts. In a list of the world's hundred largest economies, fifty are corporations. General Motors' sales revenues roughly equal the combined GNP of Tanzania, Ethiopia, Nepal, Bangladesh, Zaire, Uganda, Nigeria, Kenya, and Pakistan. In another list of the world's totalitarian and centrally managed economies, Cuba comes in seventy-third place. Seventy of the economies above her are corporations, as we have already noted. Only China, whose rulers would like to think that they can manage centrally, gets into the top set. North Korea doesn't even make the top five hundred.

The issues raised by these facts are those of accountability. These issues will push their way up the agenda of politicians and directors as the century comes to an end. When corporations are bigger than nation states you have to ask who governs them and for whom, and when those corporate states eschew democracy in favor of efficiency you have to wonder how long they will last, because history suggests that when people get richer they demand a voice. There are no rich dictatorships.

Because we did not regard a business as a community, we never thought to apply the same rules to them as we would to a nation state, where matters of human rights, free speech, and the responsibility of the governors to the governed would be argued and even fought over. If a country decided, unilaterally, to disenfranchise and expel forty thousand of its citizens, voices would be raised around the world. When a corporation such as AT&T does it, the stock price goes up and with it the earnings of its chief executive.

All this will have to change, in time. Big corporations are not multinational or transnational, they are supranational, floating free of nationalities. They are anchored in no one country, answerable to no one government. Increasingly virtual, made up of separate bits connected by electronics, they are literally hard to pin down. Their shareholdings are so dispersed and intermingled with other corporations that it is not clear who owns them, and as more and more of them start to buy back their own stock and hold it in their own treasury, the day could come when the corporation eventually owns itself.

There are some clear advantages in having supranational bodies such as businesses. They redistribute their assets around the world, bringing resources and technology to new areas. Because they are answerable only to themselves they can make bolder and quicker decisions. They can gather together finances from around the world, and build partnerships on a scale and of a type that governments on their own would find difficult if not impossible. They can apply ethical standards to the people who make the products that they buy. These supranational bodies, in sum, make things happen which otherwise would not happen. We need them.

But it does not always follow that what is good for General Motors is good for the rest of the world. Organizations of this size, which are accountable only to themselves, make governments uncomfortable. A form of governance will need to be created which represents the interests of other parties. If the organizations do not devise this form of governance for themselves they will find it imposed upon them by international pressure. Were the United Nations less obsessed with its own governance problems, this is an area to which it might usefully turn its attention. Before it does so, the big companies ought to come up with their own proposals. It may be that the concepts of citizenship and representative democracy may have more to offer than those of property rights.

The Citizen Company

B USINESSES, THEN, and indeed all institutions, are communities not properties, and their inhabitants are to be more properly thought of as citizens rather than employees or human resources. What will this mean in practice?

Citizens in all democracies have the rights of residence, justice, free speech, a share of the wealth of society in some way, and a say, usually a vote, in the governance of their society. Most importantly, however, a citizen is entitled to life, liberty, and the pursuit of happiness, the three concepts that America made the basis of democracy, in other words the right to make your own life, subject to the laws of the land. The essential freedom of the individual has been the driving force behind democracy down the ages, but it is freedom combined with commitment. If you want to pick the flowers you should help to tend the garden. Put another way, citizenship is the chance to make a difference in the place where you belong. It is this force that organizations must now come to terms with as their individuals begin to expect from their work communities the same collection of freedoms, rights, and responsibilities that they have in the wider society. People are property no more.

Translated into corporate terms, a citizen's right to residence means some guarantee of employment; not for life, because that would be unrealistic, but for a fixed period of years—a decade, for example. It is reasonable to substitute predictability for permanence in a more uncertain world, and few, anyway, of the citizen-caliber workers would want to sign a commitment for life. What is needed to restore commitment in the workplace is a rebalancing of power, so that those in control make commitments in order to win commitment. We will increasingly, I suggest, live our lives in five- to ten-year chunks, so that a ten-year commitment will be seen as a fair definition of guaranteed residence. Justice, free speech, and a share of the wealth are all easy to translate into the corporate world, but not always delivered. A say in governance translates into a right to be consulted about major decisions affecting the future of the corporation.

This has all the feel of a trade union manifesto, and some unions are moving this way, wanting to make their members citizens of the employing organization. In 1997 two large British industrial groups agreed to a guarantee of four years' employment for their core workforce in return for a promise of flexible working. A number of American corporations are negotiating similar arrangements. But citizenship is not just the outcome of negotiation or arbitration. It is more subtle than that, something that grows from a shared commitment, some of which can be defined in writing, such as the length of residence and the share of the wealth, but much of which is more intangible. As long as trade unions have an adversarial relationship with the organization they will have little role in a citizen company, and the citizens will not want them.

To an outsider, citizenship is a vital part of American life. Americans are as proud to be Americans as the Romans of old were proud to say *civis Romanus sum*—I am a Roman citizen. A common citizenship is the idea that binds such a diverse nation together in a blend of rights and obligations. Americans are rightly proud of their individuality, but they balance that with a need to belong, even to conform. The visitor can wonder how the vaunted individuality can go along with the idea of "dress-down Fridays" in which the freedom to dress casually seems to be almost a requirement to don another sort of uniform, yet it is this very acceptance of conformity as a requirement of belonging that makes it possible for such an individualist people to live together in relative harmony. It is strange, therefore, that the notions of citizenship do not extend into American corporations.

Oddly, perhaps, the British are not citizens (except, by international convention, on their passports) but subjects, subjects of Her Majesty the Queen. Although this is an historical accident, the different words may have made a subconscious difference. There is no Bill of Rights in Britain and no written constitution. Citizens tend to expect these things, which are to be found in most other democracies. The only time that the language of citizenship has been used in Britain has been in the form of the Conservative government's idea of a citizens' charter for the users of the public services. An unexceptionable idea in itself, calling it a citizens' charter made "citizen" sound like "customer," thereby degrading the whole concept of citizenship. This is a pity, because it will make it less likely that British companies will see the point of adopting the idea of corporate citizenship, except in a very loose and informal way. This may not be enough to satisfy the people whose loyalty and commitment they need to win. Citizen companies will need written constitutions.

The spirit of citizenship, however, is more important than the letter of the constitution. A state exists for its citizens, to make their lives better and more worthwhile, although it can only do this by trading profitably and peaceably with its neighbors. A democratic state, in other words, is properly selfish, looking to live up to its ideals by working with and for others. Similarly, a citizen company is primarily concerned with the betterment of its own people, although it can only do this by caring fanatically for its customers, innovating constantly, and working efficiently.

I once heard the chief executive of an advertising agency addressing the new recruits.

"What," he said, "would you say is the purpose of this agency?"

"To make money for the owners?" suggested one.

"To make our customers successful?" proffered another.

"To produce wonderful ads?" volunteered a third.

"Wrong, all wrong," said the chief, "The purpose of this agency is to enable all of us to have wonderfully fulfilling lives. In order to do that we have to work our guts out for the customers, keep our owners happy, and do wonderfully creative work, but it's in that order."

Partnership or associate are terms that fall more comfortably on corporate ears. They are also terms that are easier to apply to two other stakeholders—the suppliers and the customers. It is important for any company to win the trust and cooperation of the largest and most important of these groups, along with the most significant of their investors. Were citizenship to be formalized in any way, it would be appropriate to see these other stakeholders as associate citizens, with at least the right to be kept informed, to be consulted whenever appropriate. This form of associate citizenship should help to bond these crucial players into the long-term aims of the organization and to build a degree of mutual trust by the sharing of information. To win trust you have first to give trust.

One way to give formal expression to the right of citizenship would be to resurrect the old idea of voting and non-voting shares, often called A and B shares. The A shares, with their votes, would be confined to the personal citizens of the business—the core employees, or a trust representing their interests. To these could be added significant holders of the equity, being investors who could be presumed to have a long-term interest in the business. Citizen rights could also be extended to the larger suppliers if they held an equity stake (as suppliers tend to do in Japan). To involve the community it might be possible to create the equivalent of the "golden share" which the British Government awarded themselves in some of the companies created by privatization. This would give the community a voice, and conceivably a veto, in specific areas to do with the environment. The voting shares would not be tradable except between those who qualified for them and would be issued, in the first place, only to those who qualified for them. They would be bought back by the company if and when those owning them no longer qualified, either because they had sold their ordinary B shares, had left the company, or ceased to supply it. The point of the different types of shares is to differentiate between those who are merely betting on the company and those who have a real stake in its future. Only the latter, in fairness, should be entitled to vote on that future because those who are only there for the ride can always vote with their feet and sell their shares.

The idea of non-voting shares has always been hotly contested by the investment community—for obvious reasons. The investors would lose much of their power. But it is this power that will have to be reduced if the real members of these wealth-creating communities, the people who work there, are to have more say over their destiny and if the business is going to be more than the property of its financiers. The change will not, however, be soon or sudden. It will happen as the newer businesses explore ways to enfranchise their important constituents. It is only when these new businesses become large in their turn that the stock markets of the world will notice that they have, in their turn, lost their power.

The emergence of completely new forms of organizations may, of course, make all the talk of ownership irrelevant. The Internet, probably the fastest growing organization of all time, is owned by no one. Visa, the credit card service, carries over seven billion transactions a year, worth over $650 billion, but is "owned," if that is the right word, by the financial institutions, well over twenty thousand of them, who use its services. Organizations like the Internet and Visa are facilitating mechanisms rather than collections of assets. Few in number at the moment, they may set a pattern for the future as more and more independent operators look for Geoff Mulgan's mechanisms of "connexity."

Federalism is an old idea for the combination of independents but one which, rethought for the information age, offers some clues to possible futures. The point of federalism is that too much power should never be in one place or in one function. The center is the servant of the parts, a facilitating mechanism with powers delegated to it by those parts. In practical terms, ownership then resides with the parts even if the outside investors think they own the whole. To equate federalism with a super-state ruled by a powerful center is a uniquely British distortion, one that may haunt us in years to come if we turn our backs on what may well be the form of the future.

Multinational companies have, perforce, become federal, although they don't always call it that or recognize what they have done. The need to be both local and global, or to be what some call multi-local, has forced them to work out a form of governance that gives as much authority to the local bodies as is possible without endangering the whole. Firms like Johnson and Johnson, Coca-Cola, IBM in its new guise, the oil companies, and Asea Brown Boveri are some prime examples. The result is a system of very small centers, often less than two hundred people, concentrating on the design of the organization, its longer-term investments, and the key appointments, with a watching brief to detect any danger signs in the day-to-day operations. These day-to-day operations are, however, the responsibility of the local and frontline people and it is they who now drive the business, leaving the center to do only what it can do best on behalf of them all. The federal idea, however, of reverse delegation, from the parts to the center, does not only apply to the multinational giants. The principle applies to all levels of business. The center does not have to do everything itself. It should coordinate, not direct.

We recently installed a new kitchen in our home. The firm we went to implied that they would design, build, and install the kitchen. In practice they did none of these things themselves. It was a hollow firm. All the functions were subcontracted. None of them worked as they should. There was little the original firm could do about it other than harass and cajole their subcontractors who held the real power. It would have worked better the other way around: if the subcontractors had owned the firm who first sold us the promise of the kitchen, because it was the subcontractors who had the real power, but needed help to deliver it.

It will happen that way, eventually. Effective ownership will gradually revert to those who hold the resources, who will employ those who previously employed them. Those on the outside who provide only one of the resources—finance—will inevitably see their effective power recede. It is called "subsidiarity," the old idea that power should morally and rightly lie at the bottom not the top of things. Put more simply—stealing people's responsibilities is morally wrong and doesn't work in the end. It is a pleasing thought that, ultimately, the pressures of modern business will compel us to be moral.

Sometimes one has to wonder why we need the concept of ownership at all. Oxfam, that large non-governmental organization, was described to me as a community which belonged to no one and which was fuelled by belief. As business realizes that its best people are really volunteers, there because they want to be, not because they have to, the model of the voluntary agencies may become increasingly relevant.

THE HERDING OF CATS

Citizenship is about autonomy, the freedom to run your own life. In return for this freedom, the corporate state can demand little, but hope for much. Citizens in a democracy are free to emigrate. You cannot stop anyone leaving. Nor can you demand commitment, only hope for it. Combining this freedom and these rights with the aims of the organization is the real challenge of the citizen company. Many managers would prefer not to accept the challenge, because organizing talented people is akin to the proverbial herding of cats—difficult by definition. We have to manage people whom we can't totally control. Instead we have to trust them, and they have to trust us. The principle is simple. The practicalities mean that it seldom happens.

For a start, organizations as well as individuals have to earn the right to be trusted. But in an atmosphere of downlayering and outsourcing, loyalty to the organization is today a rare commodity. Which is odd, because loyalty is worth money. Frederick Reichfield has put numbers on the loyalty effect, suggesting that *dis*loyalty from employees, investors, and customers can stunt performance and productivity by up to 50 percent.

Once established, however, an organization with mutual trust at its core can be both creative and efficient. People obviously work better if they are not looking over their shoulders for the next job. They work more creatively if they respect the people around them and believe in what they are doing. Where they trust the organization, where they are committed to its goals and share in some way in the results of the business, they are more likely to accept relocation, reassignments, even temporary across-the-board pay cuts.

Who are these citizens? States, nowadays, require proof of talent and good behavior from those who would apply to be their citizens. Some states would like to apply similar tests to those born into their citizenship, were there only someplace else that they could dump them. Organizations are privileged in this respect. They can choose all their citizens, and would be wise to do so very carefully. Citizenship will certainly not be granted to all. In changing times no organization can make even ten-year commitments to too many people, but will keep their citizenship core as small as possible.

There will also be the necessary mercenaries, who could always turn into citizens, and there will be probationer citizens, who have to prove their worth and earn trust. The citizen core will be the proven "trusties." For an example of how such an organization works we only have to look at professional partnerships, in law, accountancy, consulting, or architecture. The partners in a professional partnership are the full citizens of that organization, so much so that all the outcomes belong to them, bad as well as good. A public company with limited liability does not have to ask so much of its citizens, but, proportionately, the rewards and the commitment are probably lower.

Businesses could also look at universities, who have long struggled with the dilemma of tenure, or life citizenship. This dilemma is nicely put in the jibe that those who need tenure don't deserve it and those who deserve it don't need it. Tenure, which was once the guarantee that you could speak your mind without fear of dismissal, is now a guarantee of a job for life, a protection that the best should not need. Unfortunately, the best are not guaranteed to remain that way. The universities fear that they may get lumbered with unworthy citizens who cannot be expelled. Indefinite tenure then becomes expensive and demoralizing to the rest.

To prevent this deterioration the stakes have been raised in the initial tenure decision. It is now much harder to be accepted as a full citizen after the necessary probationary period. Tenure is also becoming more conditional, subject to periodic review or even to termination after due process and proper notice. Citizenship, in other words, is now more clearly seen to have responsibilities as well as rights. In business it was often the other way around—citizens, if one could call them such, had more responsibilities than rights. The worlds of academia and commerce are meeting each other halfway.

The payoff for a citizen company should be a shared commitment and mutual trust. But the trust has to be in the bloodstream, no matter how well the bone structure or the nervous system has been designed. In a world where work is where you are—in the car or plane, at the office or at home, on the client's premises or in a hotel—you will increasingly have to work with people whom you do not see. Organizations are drowning in communications, in e-mail, voice-mail, faxes, and telephones, but you can tell lies on e-mail and not be noticed, and who knows whether your fax or your e-mail has actually been read, not crumpled, lost, or deleted. More than ever before we have to trust those with whom we work. Trust sounds like a nice motherhood term, something no one could be against, all warm and woolly. In practice, however, it is difficult and tough. Management by trust depends upon some clear rules and principles, which will have to become the guidebook for a citizen company. There are seven cardinal principles of trust:

1. Trust is not blind.

It is unwise to trust people whom you do not know well, whom you have not observed in action over time, and who are not committed to the same goals. How many people do any of us know that well? Perhaps more pertinently, how many people know us that well? In ordinary life there seems to be a rule of twelve. When asked how many people's deaths would affect them personally, or how many telephone numbers they can remember, it is seldom more than twelve. Work demands less stringent conditions. In practice, we can probably know a maximum of fifty people well enough to rely on them in ordinary circumstances. Those fifty can, in their turn, know another fifty, and so on.

Large organizations are not, therefore, incompatible with the principle of trust, but they have to be made up of relatively constant and smaller groupings. Impossible? Asea Brown Boveri (ABB) has 225,000 employees working in 5,000 business units which operate in 142 different countries. Each unit has an average of forty-five people working in its citizen core. The larger factories manage with three hundred, which is stretching it. The units combine with each other in an infinitely flexible way to create a powerful and fast-growing complex corporation, but the building blocks conform to the rule of fifty.

Make the groups larger, or change them too frequently, and the organization starts to replace trust with systems of control, because the people do not know each other well enough to develop trust. My title, in one large organization, was MKR/32. In this capacity I wrote memos to FIN/41 or PRO/23. I often knew no names and met no people behind those titles. I had no reason to trust them, and, frankly, no desire to. I was a "temporary role occupant" in the jargon of the time, a role occupant in an organization of command and control, based on the premise that no one could really be trusted, only the system. I left after a year, for such places can truly be a prison for the human soul, and in those prisons people seldom grow because there is no space to explore the truth about yourself. Worse, these prisons, boring though they may be, suck up energy, leaving little over for exploration outside. Role underload, studies show, can be more crippling than role overload.

2. Trust needs boundaries.

Unlimited trust is, in practice, unrealistic. We trust our friends in some areas of life, but not necessarily in all. A neighbor may be a great help in emergencies, but hopelessly unreliable when it comes to money. "I would trust him with everything—except my wife" one man wrote in a reference for an applicant to the program I was running. We manage our young on a loose rein, but the rein is always there, getting longer and looser as we trust them more. It is no different in organizations.

By trust, organizations really mean confidence, a confidence in someone's competence, and in their commitment to a goal. Define that goal, and the trusted individual or team can be left to get on with it. Control is then exercised after the event, by assessing the results, rather than before the event, by granting permission. This freedom within boundaries works best, of course, when the work unit is self-contained, with the capability of solving its own problems.

Trust-based organizations are redesigning their work, pulling back from the old reductionist models of organization, whereby everything was divided into component parts or functions, where everyone only did parts of things and seldom saw the whole. The new, holistic designs for the units of the organization look, at first, to be more expensive than the old functional types, because they often duplicate functions, maintaining separate accounting sections, for instance. The hope is that the energy and effectiveness released by the new freedom within boundaries more than compensates. Where we are trusted to find our own means to some agreed results we have the room to explore, to put our own signature on the work.

Unfortunately, this redesigning was called "re-engineering"—a word from the old world of machines. Re-engineering became a euphemism for getting rid of people, the sign of a manipulative management, never to be trusted. This is sad, because the redesigning was intended to be the outward and visible sign of trust. It is interesting to reflect that very old organizations, such as the Catholic Church, were structured on the principle of the microcosm: that each part should be a microcosm, a smaller mirror image of the whole, with the ability to organize its own destiny. Perversely, it was because the center could not communicate with the parts that the parts had to be trusted to look after themselves, bonded together only by a common ethos and tradition. Trust was then essential. These days, the abundance of our communications gets in the way of trust. It is too easy to find out what is going on.

3. Trust requires constant learning.

An organizational architecture, made up of relatively independent and constant groupings, pushes the organization towards the sort of federal structure that is becoming more common everywhere. A necessary condition of constancy, however, is an ability to change. The constant groups must always be flexible enough to change when times, and customers, demand it. This, in turn, requires that the groups keep themselves abreast of change, forever exploring new options and new technologies, in order to create a real learning culture. The choice of people for these groups is, therefore, of crucial importance. Every individual has to be capable of self-renewal. The ability to search for oneself and to regard learning as a continuing part of life, which was the justification for trusting someone in the first place, becomes one of the keys to its success.

Learning, however, like trust, can be squashed by fear. No one will stick his neck out, or take the sort of initiatives which new situations require, if they are fearful of the consequences if they are wrong. Trust, like learning, requires unconditional support, and forgiveness for mistakes, provided always that the mistakes are learnt from.

4. Trust is tough.

When trust proves to be misplaced, not necessarily because people are deceitful or malicious, but because they do not live up to expectations, or cannot be relied upon to do what is needed, then those people have, ultimately, to go, or have their boundaries severely curtailed. Trust is like glass: once broken it can never be the same again. Where you cannot trust, you have to check once more, with all the systems of control that involves. Therefore, for the sake of the bigger whole the individual must leave. Trust has to be ruthless. The pressures to perform, however, can be positive. Most of us need deadlines and targets to pull the best out of us. Where rules and checks predominate, on the other hand, satisficing, doing enough to get by, is the preferred behavior. We settle for enough when enough, in the case of personal growth or creativity, is never enough.

5. Trust needs bonding.
Self-contained units, responsible for delivering specified results, are the necessary building blocks of an organization based on trust, but long-lasting groups of "trusties" can create their own problems, those of organizations within the organization. For the whole to work, the goals of the parts have to gel with the goals of the whole. The blossoming of vision and mission statements is one attempt to deal with this, as are campaigns for "total quality" or "excellence." These well-meant initiatives can boomerang, however, if they are imposed from the top. They become the equivalent of the compulsory school song, more mocked than loved. In one organization where I worked, a memorandum was circulated from the head office stating that starting immediately, the organization was committed to a Theory Y philosophy—a belief that individuals are self-motivating. The contrast between the medium and the message caused hilarity. Like morality, visions and missions are caught, not taught.

Anita Roddick holds her spreading Body Shop group together by what can best be called "personal infection," pouring her energies into the reinforcement of her values and beliefs through every medium she can find. It is always a dangerous strategy to personalize a mission, in case the person herself stumbles or falls, but organizations based on trust need this sort of personal statement from their leaders. Trust is not, and never can be, an impersonal commodity.

6. *Trust needs touch.*

Visionary leaders, however, no matter how articulate, are not enough. A shared commitment still requires personal contact to make the commitment feel real. Paradoxically, the more virtual an organization becomes the more its people need to meet in person. The meetings, however, are different. They are more to do with process than task, more concerned that the people get to know each other than that they deliver. Video conferences are more task-focused, but they are easier and more productive if the individuals already know each other as persons, not just as images on the screen. Work and play, therefore, alternate in many of the corporate get-togethers which now fill the conference resorts out of season.

These are not perks for the privileged. They are the necessary lubricants of virtuality, occasions for not only getting to know each other, and for meeting the leaders, but for reinforcing corporate goals and rethinking corporate strategies. As one who delivers the occasional "cabaret" at such occasions, I am always surprised to find how few of the participants have met each other in person, even if they have worked together before. I am then further surprised by how quickly a common mood develops. You can almost watch the culture grow and you wonder how anyone could have worked effectively without it.

7. *Trust has to be earned.*

This principle is the most obvious and yet the most neglected. Organizations who expect their people to trust them must first demonstrate that they are trustworthy. Organizations that break implied contracts through downsizing will find that those who are left will trust them less. Individuals will not be trusted fully until they have proved that they can deliver. Governments who

THE CITIZEN COMPANY   187

promise to cut taxes but end up increasing them forfeit the trust
of the voters.

These cultures of trust are easier to grow and to preserve
within the bounds of a single organization. As organizations become semi-dismantled, as many more people find themselves
outside the organization, then the issues of trust become more
difficult to deal with. Do you and your suppliers, or you and your
clients, have the same goals? If not, then trust will be difficult
because each will suspect the other of promoting their agenda
rather than the joint one. Are the boundaries and the contracts
clear and understood? How often have you met, and what sort of
affinity is there between you? Are genuine mistakes acknowl-
edged and accepted? These questions are as important outside
the organization as inside. If they can't be answered positively,
business becomes adversarial, complicated, and no fun.

FOUR STORIES TO MAKE A POINT

St. Luke's

St. Luke's is a strange name for an advertising agency, but
then St. Luke's is a strange place. A breakaway or, as they prefer
to call it, an earn-out from Omnicom, the giant U.S. marketing
services group, the founders were the London end of Chiat/Day
before it was taken over by Omnicom. At the end of 1996 there
were fifty-five names on their notepaper, because that was the
number of staff they had then. They were on the notepaper
because the agency is owned by all members of the staff, from
receptionist to chairman.

The ownership is handled through a British device called a
"Quest"—a qualifying employee share ownership trust. The trust

held all the shares initially, but then dispensed some of them to each employee. Every year there is another distribution so that those who stay longest get the most shares. The company is valued every year and the trust buys back, at full value, the shares of anyone who is leaving, although not many are expected to leave, says Andy Law, the chairman. In fact, unusually for the advertising industry, only two of the original thirty-five members in 1995 have since left, one to be a deep sea diver.

Although everyone is an equal citizen, as far as their owner-ship entitlement goes, the normal operational hierarchies do still exist, but they are as flat as can be. There are also pay differen-tials and annual performance reviews. The office is modelled on a university, in the sense that the place is a resource center rather than a working-day apartment house. There is a refectory and a library, but no personal offices, and no one has a secretary, not even the chairman. Staff put their belongings in lockers and carry their work around in standard-issue shoulder bags, borrow-ing an office or a desk when they need it. Each floor has com-puters where messages and diaries can be checked. The rooms are, in fact, allocated to clients rather than departments. Once a room has been allocated to a client, all meetings and data rele-vant to that client are held there. Andy Law tells clients, "Here is a raw, boiling talent of creative people who are smart and have got the right resources. You tell us what you need and we'll change to fit the shape."

Not to everyone's taste perhaps, but here is a new model of a citizenship company, where everyone is involved and committed to a common purpose, which is underlined by the physical lay-out. Why, after all, are we so fixated on having our private apart-ment at work? Most people work where the client is—teachers don't have private offices, nor do plumbers, electricians, or al-most anyone in the building trade. Shop assistants, restaurant staff, hairdressers, most journalists, actors, consultants most of the time, truck drivers, gardeners and cooks, factory foremen and -women—none of these feels the need for a private space which they can fill with their files and their family photographs. They find their privacy at home, if they need it.

More and more of us will be pressured into doing likewise as organizations begin to question the sense of having offices available for 168 hours a week but only used for 48 or so at most. We will turn the idea of the office upside down, as St. Luke's has done, and make the office the client's room so that we work together where the client is, and on our own wherever we want to be.

Making Magic

As an experiment in executive development, the Arts Business Forum in London invited ten leading companies to nominate one of their executives to join an experimental program of learning from the theater. Each executive was asked to choose a minimum of four theater performances from the extensive program of foreign theater and dance put together by the London International Festival of Theater over six weeks. The idea was that they should watch the show, meet the director and the cast, and foregather for a one-day seminar at the end of the festival to discuss what, if anything, they had learned.

Six of them went to the circus as one of their chosen shows. It was a special circus from France. No animals, only humans performing extraordinary feats on the trapeze, with knives, flaming torches, complicated and unbelievable group acrobatics, all done with flair and precision. At the seminar they said that they had seldom seen such an example of teamwork, discipline, and commitment to excellence—better, said one, than anything in our company. One of them summed it up: "That night, we saw ordinary people making magic," and he added, "I bet they are paid peanuts, while my bank pays people fortunes and we don't get anything like that standard of work out of them. What are we missing?"

What they were missing, the group agreed, was a dedication to an art form which mattered more to them than money, plus the nightly applause which was a constant recognition of their expertise and their "magic." Large pay packets and an annual appraisal do not always compensate for that intensity of commitment or the nightly "high" for the whole team.

The circus is one example of what businesses can learn from other organizations who have long experience of harnessing individual talent to common purposes. Professionalism, projects, passion, and pride seem to be the hallmarks of the organizations of talent. The theater is another example, one where individuals become team members for a production, with a shared interest in its success. In like vein, the world of film and television is organized around projects and, at its best, draws on passion and pride as well as professionalism. Orchestras and jazz bands have also been cited as models for the new way of working. Few of these places would claim to be perfect, but they understand that at their best they are engaged in making magic.

X Inc.

This hi-tech business in Silicon Valley, California, worked to a different philosophy. It was fourteen years old in 1995, with sales growing at a compound rate of 30 percent, and a workforce of talented young people, slowly growing older, most of them shareholders but not citizens. The difference was crucial. They set up a task force to plot their way into the future.

"What is the objective of the company?" I asked them when they came to see me.

"To make as much money as possible," they said.

"For whom?"

"For the shareholders, of course, but we are also shareholders. It is exciting—we check the share price in the morning, again at lunchtime, and then before we go home in the evening, and calculate how much richer we have become during the day. Every member of this group is a millionaire several times over."

"What do you spend it on?" I asked, curious.

"There isn't time to spend it, we are too busy making it!"

"So what's the problem?"

"Well, as we get bigger, it gets ever harder to keep up the percentage growth rate which the stock market expects, so the share price has fallen. Added to which, as we bring more people in, we have to share more of the equity with them, so, as we get bigger, we get rich more slowly, may even get less rich if the shares keep falling. We are also, if we are honest, feeling rather tired, although we're still young, but the pressure gets greater all the time. We don't have a training budget because there's no time for training—we just hire the expertise we need when we need it, and, because there's no room for mistakes, we get rid of anyone if they get it wrong at any time. There is therefore a very tense atmosphere in the organization and a reluctance to take initiative."

I asked them to name the company they would most like to be like. They named their near neighbor, a world name as an organization, universally respected, whose growth rate, as a mature business, was much slower than theirs, with much lower dividends paid to stockholders.

"Given your aims," I said, "that example doesn't make much sense."

After some discussion they admitted that what they admired about their neighbor was what it stood for as a company, the way it treated its people, its determination to build for a long-term future. That company had obviously persuaded the stock market to accept a relatively moderate rate of return in exchange for a promise of long-term growth and profitability.

The group started, then, to talk about their real pride in what they did: their technological prowess, the way their products made things possible which had never been dreamed of, the fun of going, technologically, where no one had ever been before, even in imagination. They told stories of how the equipment they made had saved lives, had helped to revolutionize education in poor countries, and how it could bring government closer to people everywhere. They told me, in other words, of their dream and of what they thought was the real purpose of their existence, the essence or soul of the company. The money part was the scorecard. How you read it depended on what game you thought you were playing.

They went away pondering a different idea of the company, and a different future. The combination of a sense of personality or soul, with a long-term purpose or dream; with an agreed understanding of "enough" by shareholders and managers alike in terms of what a decent return on their capital would be; of time to invest in the people who would be their future and an atmosphere that trusted each to do their best and to learn from any mistakes, was, they realized, a combination that they could wish for themselves. Maximizing, after a while, becomes self-defeating. "Enough" now is essential for "more" in the future, provided you know where that future is. Greed can get in the way of growth. Citizens want a future as well as present dividends.

The Great Game of Business

This is the title of a book written by Jack Stack, describing his experience at Springfield Re-Manufacturing Company in Missouri. This company has now become as much an exhibition as a manufacturing business. More than 2,500 people have paid $1,250 each to go and see what Jack Stack and his colleagues have been doing in this un-hi-tech business, reconditioning engines. The concept which they gave birth to and called "open book management" may be the most important of the new managerial gizmos of recent times, with the added value that it corresponds with common sense and a respect for the average human being's capacity for good work if he or she is treated as a citizen.

In 1983 Stack and others bought out a unit of International Harvester when that company was going through hard times. They started with no money and lots of debt, to be precise, an 89:1 debt to equity ratio with interest at 18 percent. Stack's only priority, he says, was "don't run out of cash." To help with that aim it was important to help all the 119 people working at Springfield Re-Manufacturing to understand the firm's cash situation, so the management started to share all the numbers with everyone, right down to the doorman, and to provide bonus systems and share incentives to reward their efforts. Over 30 percent of the company is now owned by the workers. All obvious, really, but more difficult than one might think to do in practice. You have to walk your talk, as they say.

The process begins by giving people information regularly, every week, on company performance, as if they were confidential analysts looking at the business. Job counts, inventory levels, sales, expense ratios, bank balances—nothing is held back. The company then puts a great deal of effort into educating people to understand all these numbers. There are what they call "huddles" to share views and to help work out the implications of the financial figures, a network of "player coaches," and a big emphasis on self-management. Stack called it The Great Game of Business, on the grounds that business can be fun and personally rewarding, like a good game, but that to play it everyone needs to know all the rules; they need to be able to follow the action, and they have to have a stake in winning.

Denise Bredfeld remembers her first experience with this business philosophy. She worked on the line building pumps, valves, and cylinders. Jack asked her one day if she thought that she was making the company money.

"Sure," she replied.

"Prove it," said Jack.

"Then he gave me a two-hour lecture on how to determine costs. I took two weeks and scrabbled around, digging up information. I didn't know anything. I had to learn as I went along. Finally I proved that our section was making money, but not as much as I thought. Transmissions were making more. They say numbers don't lie—and it was obvious from the numbers what we had to do. He armed us with the information we needed to make wise decisions."

Some of the proof lies in the numbers. The share price rose from 10 cents to $18.60 in just ten years. The company now does over $100 million in sales, operates several different divisions, and employs nearly 800 people. Jack wrote his book about it all, and has now had more than two hundred imitators. Treating people as responsible adults and citizens, trust and recognition, room to be yourself—it seems to work, for everyone.

The stories cited relate to relatively small organizations. At first sight it is hard to see how they might apply to the large supranationals discussed in the previous chapter. But, as ABB has proved, large organizations can be composed of flexible combinations of very small organizations, in each of which there can be a sense of partnership in a shared adventure, trust, recognition, and a share in the rewards of success. The four p's of professionalism, projects, passion, and pride are not the exclusive property of new or creative businesses, but they seem to be the necessary elements of corporate citizenship. Given the mood of the times, and the hungry spirit which sits within each of us, there is no alternative but to give more space and more sense of partnership to the citizen core of any organization.

The practical implications are:

—a much greater emphasis on the selection of the citizens, to ensure that they are likely to be kindred spirits, as well as professionally competent;

—an explicit contract with each individual, laying down tenure limits and partnership rights, to demonstrate that the work is to the benefit of all, and to make the commitment of the organization clear;

—a formal constitution which sets out rights and duties, so that the boundaries of trust are known;

—a clear understanding, not necessarily in writing, of the imperatives of the organization, what it stands for and what it seeks to achieve, above and beyond the monetary goals, to elicit some of that passion;

—control by results more than by procedures, as a demonstration of trust and a source of pride.

Those who qualify for the citizen core of any organization will no longer be content to be regarded as the instruments of that organization, no matter how well rewarded, because they will, mostly, be able to turn mercenary if they need to. The citizen company will, therefore, gradually become a necessary way to organize, difficult though it will always be to manage and to lead.

In a recent book, *Organizing Genius,* Warren Bennis, philosopher of leadership and articulate observer of American organizations, has described the methods and the history of some of

America's most famous creative groups, including the Manhattan Project which made the first atomic bomb, the Disney animation studio, and Bill Clinton's campaign team for his first presidential election. As he analyzes these great groups, Bennis finds they had much in common despite their variety. They were all grouped around a specific and prestigious project and their members were all recognized as experts in their field. Those members had a consuming passion for their cause. They were unconcerned about money or material comfort, often working in makeshift quarters for long hours with little pay, they were young (mostly under thirty), had great camaraderie, and were given as much space in their work as they could handle. Their pride in their membership and, eventually, their achievements were obvious. Bennis doesn't call them citizens, but that is what, in effect, they were.

These great groups did not last forever. Immortality seemed beyond their grasp, possibly because they were defined around projects with a beginning and an end, rather than a community made up of projects. Their members probably never had as intense an experience again, nor is it given to all of us to be part of such groups, but they will have provided their members with a taste of what it is to make magic, and the rest of us with lessons in how to herd the cats in the cause of something memorable.

A Proper Education

THE PHILOSOPHY of proper selfishness has to start early. We need an approach to education which fosters responsibility for oneself and others. *How* we learn then becomes as important as *what* we learn, as I was to discover in my own education.

I left school and the university with my head packed full of knowledge; enough of it, anyway, to pass all the examinations that were put in my path. It was, naturally, a rather partial sort of knowledge, containing nothing at all of the natural sciences, or of languages other than Latin and Greek. In those days, it was thought that you could not reach the standards required of you in your chosen field *and* be, at the same time, conversant with all the other fields of study. I was, however, considered by my teachers and my parents to be a well-educated young man.

Unusually for that time, I went into industry. "You are the first member of our family to go into trade," my great-aunt said, with a disapproving sniff. But work was the stuff of life and "industry," or the business of making and selling useful things or services, was an important part of that work, whatever my relatives might feel. As a well-educated young man I rather expected my work to be a piece of cake, something at which my intellect would allow me to excel without undue effort. School and schooling were behind me, thank God, and life could now begin, and life, I felt, was for living, with all the good things that that implied.

It came as something of a shock, therefore, to encounter the world outside for the first time, and to realize that I was woefully ill-equipped, not only for the necessary business of earning a living, but, more importantly, for coping with all the new decisions which came my way, in both life and work. My first employers put it rather well: "You have a well-trained but empty mind," they told me, "which we will now try to fill with something useful, but don't imagine that you will be of any real value to us for the first ten years." I was fortunate to have lighted upon an employer prepared to invest so much time in what was, in effect, my real education, and I shall always feel guilty that I left them when the ten years were up.

A well-trained mind is not to be sneezed at, but I was soon to discover that my mind had been trained to deal with closed problems, whereas most of what I now had to deal with were open-ended problems. "What is the cost of sales?" is a closed problem, one with a right or a wrong answer. "What should we do about it?" is an open problem, one with any number of possible answers. Trained in analysis, I had no experience of taking decisions which might or might not turn out to be good. Knowing the right answer to a question, I came to realize, was not the same as making a difference in a situation, which was what I was supposed to be paid for. Worst of all, the real open-ended question—"What is all this in aid of?"—was beginning to nudge at my mind.

I had been educated in an individualist culture. My scores were mine. No one else came into it, except as competitors in some imagined race. I was on my own in the learning game at school and at the university. Not so in my work, I soon realized. Nothing happened there unless other people cooperated. How to win friends and influence people was not a course in my curriculum. Unfortunately, it was to prove essential in my new life. Being an individual star would not help me much if it was in a failing group. A group failure brought me down along with the group. Our destinies were linked, which meant that my classmates were now colleagues, not competitors. Teams were something I had encountered on the sports field, not in the classroom. They were in the box marked "fun" in my mind, not the one marked "work" or even "life." My new challenge, I discovered, was to merge these three boxes. I had discovered, rather later than most, the necessity of others. It was the start of my real education.

"So you're a university graduate are you?" said my new sales manager. "In classics, is it? I don't think that that is going to impress our Chinese salesmen! How do you propose to win their respect since you will be in charge of some of them very shortly?" Another open-ended problem! I had never before been thrust among people very different from me, with different values and assumptions about the way the world worked, or should work. I had not even met anyone more than two years older, except for relatives and teachers. Cultural exploration was a process unknown to me, and I was not accustomed to being regarded as stupid and ignorant, which I undoubtedly was, in all the things that mattered in their world. It was my first realization that there is more than one way of being intelligent.

My education, I decided then, had been positively disabling. So much of the content of what I had learned was irrelevant, while the process of learning had cultivated a set of attitudes and behaviors which were directly opposed to what seemed to be needed in real life. Although I had studied philosophy I hadn't applied it to myself. I had assumed that the point of life was obvious: to get on, get rich, get a wife, and get a family. It was beginning to be clear that life wasn't as simple as that. What I believed in, what I thought was worth working for, and with whom—these things were becoming important. So was my worry about what I personally could contribute that might not only earn me money but also make a useful contribution somewhere.

It would be nice to think that this sort of experience could not happen now, that our schools, today, prepare people much better for life and for the work which is so crucial to a satisfactory life. But I doubt it. The subjects may appear to be a little more relevant, but we are still left to learn about work at work, and about life by living it. That will always be true, but we could, I believe, do more to make sure that the *process* of education had more in common with the processes of living and working as they are today, so that the shock of reality is less cruel. I would have more faith in a national curriculum if it were to be more concerned with process than with content, and had as much to do with values and people as with knowledge and things.

The U.S. National Center for Clinical Infant Programs recently listed the seven qualities which children need to do well at school, and probably in life, I would add. They are: confidence, curiosity, intentionality, self-control, relatedness, and the capacity to communicate and to cooperate. In addition, the capacity for deferred gratification turns out to be a better definition of success than IQ. Daniel Goleman bundles all these attributes into what he calls "emotional intelligence." The success of his recent book of this title suggests that a lot of people agree. It is unfortunate that no curriculum lists these capacities as prerequisites. When I inquired of a professor of English what his course did to inculcate these qualities at the higher levels of education, given that they were largely ignored at the earlier stages, he replied, "They come here to read English, and that is exactly what they do. These other things they will have to pick up in the streets."

Schools are charged by society with multiple functions, which is one of their problems, but they are the only safe practice grounds for life that we have. They are, for that reason, precious and protected places, but they need to be clear about the implications. The economic historian R.H. Tawney, returning to Britain after the catastrophic experience of World War I and what he called a world of graves, asked for an education that was "generous, inspiring, and humane" to replace an existing system which was "neither venerable, like a college, nor popular, like a public house, but merely indispensable, like a pillar-box." He decried an approach that was narrowly utilitarian because of its "spiritual crassness" and declared that "only those institutions are loved which touch the imagination." We have still to create those places in most of our societies.

A school for life and work should, I suggest, subscribe to the following propositions, if it is to help its students begin to take responsibility for their lives, for their beliefs about the world, and for the others with whom they work or live or meet, as well as touch their imaginations and inspire their souls.

1. The discovery of oneself is more important than the discovery of the world.

Both are important, of course, but the world will always be there. We need to build up a belief in our competence to deal with it.

Too many people experience school as a failure experience, leaving with their self-esteem in tatters, believing that they are stupid, inadequate, and incapable. This is the worst possible starting point from which to begin looking for work or coping with life on one's own, particularly when so much of that work will, in future, have to be created by ourselves. By the turn of the century, it is now clear, less than half of the British workforce will be in full-time long-term jobs. We can no longer rely on our work institutions to fill our empty minds with their skills.

"Look for customers, not jobs," I told my own children when they left college—because only if you can make or do something that other people will pay you money for will you ultimately be employable. But that requires self-confidence, a saleable skill or competence, and social skills of quite a high order. It is not easy to sell one's own goods or services. It should be a guarantee to all children, as a right, that they will have these three components of survival by the time they leave school, for they are the building blocks of self-esteem, the start on the road to a full identity. If the children leave without them, it is the school that has failed.

Nelson Mandela said in his inaugural address: "Our deepest fear is not that we are inadequate, our deepest fear is that we are powerful beyond measure. We ask ourselves, 'Who am I to be brilliant, gorgeous, talented, and fabulous?' Actually, who are you not to be? You are a child of God. We are born to manifest the glory of God that is within us. It's not just in some of us, it's in everyone."

This sentiment, whether put in a religious context or not, should be one of the articles of belief of a school for life and work. We can do many things to bring it about. We can, for instance, look for ways to give every young person a success experience of some sort every year. That will be easier if the second proposition is adopted.

2. *Everyone is good at something.*

Howard Gardner, a professor of education at Harvard University, once produced a list of seven different intelligences. The idea that intelligence is so multi-dimensional was a revelation to educationalists, although on reflection it is obvious. To his list we can now add Daniel Goleman's concept of emotional intelligence. But even without these academic aids we can all make our own list, from our own experience. As time goes by, my own list grows longer as I encounter new examples of intelligence or talent. This is my current list, with the important proviso that the different intelligences need not, indeed usually do not, correlate. Fortunate are they who have more than three. All of them, however, can be developed, but those that are naturally there will develop faster.

FACTUAL INTELLIGENCE—the know-it-all facility of the encyclopedia.

ANALYTIC INTELLIGENCE—the ability to reason and to conceptualize.

NUMERATE INTELLIGENCE—being at ease with numbers of all sorts.

A combination of these first three intelligences will get you through most tests and examinations and entitle you to be called clever. But there is more to intelligence than these.

LINGUISTIC INTELLIGENCE—a facility with language and languages, even if one talks nonsense in all of them, which can happen if this intelligence is not aligned with the others.

SPATIAL INTELLIGENCE—an ability to see patterns in things. Artists, entrepreneurs, and system analysts have this ability, but often do poorly in tests of the first three intelligences. They therefore fail at school but can prosper in later life if their self-esteem is not too dented.

ATHLETIC INTELLIGENCE—although some might prefer to call it

talent, the skill of athletes is a recognizable form of intelligence, still too easily dismissed as a leisure activity. We mock some American universities for offering athletic scholarships, but perhaps they are only extending the concept of education and intelligence as they, and we, should.

INTUITIVE INTELLIGENCE—an aptitude for sensing and seeing what is not immediately obvious. Often opposed to analytic intelligence, making it difficult for the two to communicate. "You have won the argument, but I'm right," says my wife on occasion, and she usually is, because her intuitive intelligence gets it right more often than my analytic approach.

EMOTIONAL INTELLIGENCE—self-awareness and self-control, persistence, zeal, and self-motivation are often more important in life than any other faculty. Goleman quotes Aristotle: "Anyone can become angry—that is easy. But to be angry with the right person, to the right degree, for the right purpose, at the right time, and in the right way—this is not easy."

PRACTICAL INTELLIGENCE—Often called common sense, the ability to recognize what needs to be done and what can be done. The person who gets on with it, while everyone else is debating what should be done.

INTERPERSONAL INTELLIGENCE—the ability to get things done with and through others. Sometimes called social intelligence, or elevated to leadership skills, this intelligence is crucial to success and survival at work.

MUSICAL INTELLIGENCE—easy to recognize, whether in opera singers, pianists, or pop groups, this intelligence seems pleasingly unrelated to age, which means that it is an important route to success experiences for the young.

The list could, and no doubt will, continue, because there may well be other categories of intelligence. The precise names of the various intelligences are not important. What matters is the message behind the list: that these many and varied intelligences or abilities are all resources that we can use to contribute to the world, to earn a living, and to make a difference. It cannot be proved beyond a doubt, but it is a reasonable assumption that everyone starts off endowed to some degree with at least one of these intelligences. Nor is it obvious, looking at people in later life, that any particular set of intelligences is more important than any other. Any one of them can be developed to be the basis of self-respect, a successful life, and useful work.

It should be the first duty of a school for life to help the young person build up an "intelligence profile," then to encourage him or her to develop the preferred set of those intelligences, and to work out how best to employ them. This will provide the basis for that self-confidence without which little learning can occur. The development of the other intelligences can come later. A narrow focus on the first three intelligences in this list runs the risk of labelling as stupid those who do not shine in those particular intelligences but who have undoubted capacities in the other areas. That is to cheat them of a life.

The delivery of these first two propositions might seem very teacher intensive, focusing as they do on the unique qualities of each individual. But perhaps our teacher/student ratios are the wrong way round. Instead of focusing on individuals in the early years of life, we provide the attention when they really should not need it at all. Thus we have thirty pupils or more to a teacher in a primary school, but ten or fewer in higher education. These numbers ought to be reversed, in which case we would need, theoretically, no more teachers in total, and they would probably cost less.

Sir Christopher Ball, the Director of Learning at the Royal Society for the Encouragement of Arts, Manufactures, and Commerce in London, has a neat formula for these ratios—take the age of the pupil and multiply by two. Five-year-olds would then get one teacher for every ten pupils, while twenty-year-olds at university would have one teacher for every forty students, but by then they should be independent learners. There obviously can't be a straight swap of professors for primary teachers, so an initial investment will be needed at the primary end while we stretch the ratios at the university level. That stretch is going to happen anyway as the numbers attending university continue to rise, probably without any accompanying rise in resources.

On the campus of Tufts University in the U.S.A. you will find the Eliot-Pearson Preschool and Project Spectrum, a curriculum that deliberately sets out to cultivate a wide range of intelligences. It was inspired by the work of Howard Gardner. Daniel Goleman watched four-year-old Judy there. To the casual observer she was a shy, withdrawn kid, not joining in the action at playtime, always on the margin of activities. Yet when Judy's teacher asked her to match each boy and girl with their favorite playmates, Judy did so with complete accuracy. She had a perfect social map of her class and a level of perceptiveness unusual for any four-year-old. It was a skill which might allow her to blossom into a star later on in life, in people-sensitive fields such as diplomacy, marketing, or management. In a more traditional school such a talent would have been ignored, and Judy classified as socially inadequate. Her self-respect would have been dented, possibly for life.

3. Life is a marathon, not a horse race.
In a horse race only the first three count. The rest are also-rans. In a marathon everyone who completes the course is a winner. While some run faster than others and some compete with others up at the front, most of the runners are running against themselves, seeking to better the standards which they set them-

selves. Life is more like a marathon for most of us. We choose which races to enter, and what pace to run at, seeking, most of the time, to better ourselves. There is ultimately no winning and losing, only the taking part, and the getting better.

Compulsory tests at seven, eleven, fourteen, and sixteen, as in Britain, turn education into a horse race, not a marathon, because the scores, however objective they are intended to be, inevitably label the young person as below or above average. Comparative grading at set ages turns education into a sorting device, not a development process. Although some may respond creatively to the news that they are below average in some aspect of their work, most young people turn away immediately to find some other area where they might have better luck, preferably one outside the remit of their school. America has partially avoided this trap by not having a set of uniform national tests, but within individual schools and, informally, within social groups, students are still compared one with another according to their ages. Parents and teachers would do well to remember the obvious fact that people develop at different paces.

If we ran our driving tests with compulsory once-only tests on everyone's seventeenth birthday, passing only those who were average or above, we should undoubtedly have safer roads with better and fewer drivers, but we would have disenfranchised, for life, nearly half the population. Yet that is what we, in Britain, are doing with our school examinations. This is immoral in a democratic society, because it deprives late developers of the chance of a proper selfishness.

The odd thing is that we already have a model of graded examinations in Britain which is highly regarded, one with high standards but almost universal pass rates. I refer to the system of music examinations which pupils take only when their teacher estimates that they have a good chance of passing. These examinations are not age dependent—you take them when you are ready for them. They are the appropriate examinations for a marathon as opposed to a horse race and replicate the sort of hurdles that people will encounter later in life, leaping them when they are ready for them.

Tim Brighouse, the Director of Education in Birmingham, calls these examinations "Just-in-Time Examinations." A young person should always have something to aim at, but something attainable, something retakeable, something which he or she can hold up as a mark of their achievement, irrespective of age. Adult life is not as ageist as schools are, where the month of one's birthday can be of crucial importance. These kinds of just-in-time hurdles ought to be part of the ambience in a proper school for life.

4. Knowing "what" is not as important as knowing "where," "how," and "why."

Implicit in my education was the assumption that the objective of education and training was to fill my mind with as much information as possible, so that it would be there when I needed it. Of course, I forgot most of it. In life and in work, we learn things when we need them, not before we need them. Knowledge, for most people, has a very short sell-by date. Unless it is used very quickly it goes off. That is why it is very difficult to learn a foreign language in absentia, as it were. If the new words and phrases do not get used within days, they evaporate.

Knowledge, these days, is readily available, whether it be contained in books and manuals, on CD-ROMs or in cyberspace, or in other people's experience. The trick is not to try to transfer it all to one's own brain, but to know where to find it, how to access it, and what to do with it when you have it. We need early practice in doing this. As part of their role as practice grounds for life, schools ought not to be force-feeding their students, but teaching them how to feed themselves. Original thought, I sometimes console myself, often goes with a bad memory. An overstuffed brain has less need to work things out for itself.

This changes the role of the teacher. Instead of being the sole repository of knowledge, which has traditionally been the source of their authority, teachers will have to be prepared to encourage their students to search for facts and theories in the depths of the Internet, often ending up knowing more about something than the teacher. The realization that one can outgun the expert is exciting in itself for any young person, something that a self-confident teacher should take pleasure in. The real job of the teacher is to set the task which requires the search for the knowledge, to help the individual or the group to seek it out, and to demonstrate how the knowledge can be used. The Maori language, I was told, uses the same word for teaching and learning. Perhaps they know something that we have forgotten.

Some starting skills are needed by all students, of course. A facility with words, numbers, and emotions is essential. We may not need to write, or even to type, in a future where we will talk into a computer and watch the words being spelled out in any language we choose, on the screen, but we will have to read, speak, preferably in more than one language, and be able to answer a telephone. In a digital world, where much information will come in the form of numbers, it is crucial that we are all at ease with those numbers from an early stage, and can understand how numbers relate to each other. More importantly, we need to learn how to manage our emotions, in Daniel Goleman's sense of the word, to develop self-awareness, self-control, empathy, and the arts of listening, resolving conflicts, and cooperation. And, crucially, we need to have learned how to learn, and to enjoy the process. Schools that kill that enjoyment can damage our life chances.

Those who have the appropriate native intelligences will have an easier start, but a good school can do a lot to develop these skills and abilities in all its students, starting at a very early age. Self Science, for instance, is a core curriculum subject at one San Francisco school, tailored to helping the young students understand their feelings and how they impact on other people. In a downtown school in New Haven the Social Competence Program tries to do the same for a student body that is mostly black and Hispanic. If, however, the students can learn social competence and the other skills by using them in their normal classes while working on a task which they find fun and interesting, then the learning will be less likely to "go off."

In this respect, we should remember the arts, particularly the performing arts. Theater, dance, and music allow young people to experiment with their emotions in a safe context. Besides, they make learning fun. I watched a young drama teacher at work in a primary school in the middle of one of the townships in South Africa. She had been asked to demonstrate the teaching of English, their second language, through drama. She gave those six-year-old children a range of roles in a street market and asked them to improvise, to act out their roles, using only English, asking her if they needed to know a particular word. There were forty small children in that class. I watched carefully and everyone spoke, often many at once, as is the nature of street markets. At the end of the hour-long class all the children spontaneously applauded.

The energy and enthusiasm in that classroom were infectious. The only people who missed out on the enthusiasm were the regular teachers watching the demonstration. At first these teachers tried to make the children keep quiet because noise always interfered with learning, as they thought. When they realized how much the children were learning from the role playing the teachers became nervous. The change from the traditional ways of the classroom was too threatening to the way they saw themselves.

5. School should be like work, and vice versa.
Visiting a range of schools some years back, I would often start by asking how many people worked there. I always got a response in the tens—ten or twenty, maybe, or seventy, if it was a large school. The teachers always left out the children in their counting. The children, I came to realize, were not seen as workers, but as the products of these human factories, taken in as raw material, processed, inspected, and graded, before being placed on the market.

It was a depressing thought, but it provoked me to think about what would happen if we treated the children as the real workers in an enlightened factory of creativity, with the teachers as the consultants and senior managers. Work would be organized around tasks to be done. Most of the work would be carried out in small teams or groups. There would be competition between groups but cooperation within them. The tasks would be as real as possible, but with opportunities for skill improvement and information gathering built into the timetable.

Accountability and responsibility would then become live concepts, with consequences, because it would be the students, as well as the teachers, who would have to live with those consequences. They would learn that if you turn up late for work, aren't properly prepared, or are too tired to do your best, it isn't just yourself whom you are letting down, but the whole of your group. No one is an island, maybe, but you don't believe it until you experience it.

Learning would then be seen to be the necessary ingredient for better performance on the tasks. The students would learn that it is a combination of different talents that makes things happen, and that the discovery and harnessing of these talents is critical. Older students would work with younger ones, for part of the time at least, and would have responsibilities appropriate to their relative seniority and competencies.

Our young son had the gift of an excellent treble voice. He joined a distinguished cathedral choir. Young boys like him were full working members of the choir and were treated as such. His performance in that choir was exemplary, while his work in the more traditional parts of the school syllabus was very patchy. I asked his choirmaster what the secret was—how did he get such good results where others failed? "It's simple," he said. "What we do is work, what the others do is school. He takes work seriously because we take him seriously."

Music of all sorts is one thing that young people often do as well as many adults. Their musical work, and it is work, requires discipline, practice, and high standards. Project, professionalism, pride, and passion are all there when they are working on a performance. The audience, not their teachers or their parents, are their judges. It is not school. Work may never be as satisfying again, but the young performers have had a taste of what it might be. Their self-confidence will have benefited as well.

The proposition that schools should be more like work organizations could and should be taken further. Work organizations now concentrate their own resources on their "core task," bringing in other specialists to do what they can do better. Schools have gone down this route only to the extent of contracting out the catering and the maintenance. They could go much further if they saw themselves, principally, as the designers and managers of a young person's development, not as the only teachers. Schools can't, and shouldn't, do everything. Practical skills such as word processing and computing, driving, first aid, languages, home management, money management, and presentation skills, could all be done, on contract, by specialists, leaving the teachers free to concentrate on the more general education and development of the child.

Technical skills are best learned, as in Germany, in the workplace, but this can be seen as an adjunct to the school and as part of education, to be monitored and arranged by the school. The work of society, and the values and norms of the world around us are also best learned by working in and with the surrounding community, on assignments and placements arranged by the school. Turning the workplace into a school for youngsters is not always a solution welcomed by those who run the workplace, but they may come to realize that early education is better and cheaper than later remedial education. If the skills and attitudes needed for work are best learned at work, then the workplace will have to get involved, not as an ultimate destination, but as part of the learning process.

A better spread of responsibilities for schooling between work and school would allow the schools to concentrate on what they do best. Fewer core staff, better paid and achieving more, is the formula for productivity in industry, realized by getting others to do what they do better and more efficiently. If schools adopted the same formula, they could pay teachers better and see them regain the esteem which has sometimes been lacking in the recent past, because they would be doing what they alone can do—designing the development programs of their students. It was once said of the Education Act of 1944 that it was the greatest confidence trick ever played on the British parent, in that it suggested that schools would be responsible for the development of their children. That never was true, and never could be true, but it allowed everyone else to leave the task to the school. It is time to reverse the assumption and to give the actual school a smaller but crucial role in the education of our young.

There has always been a lot of learning going on in society, but most of it has happened outside of school. We ought not to regret that, but we should capitalize on it.

6. Life is a journey, which starts at home.

I have argued that life, for most people, is a process of discovery—of who we are, what we can do, and, ultimately, why we exist and what we believe. It is a circular process, because when we discover what we are capable of and work out why we exist, it changes the way we see ourselves, which can send us off in new directions, discovering new capacities and new reasons for our existence. This spiralling journey is the true meaning of lifelong learning, and it remains, for those who pursue it, an endlessly fascinating experience, one which enriches not only the individual but all those around. Those who have tired of the journey have tired of life. They come across as dull and boring, and can soon infect their friends and colleagues with their apathy.

The best way to learn how to travel is to start travelling, with experienced travellers to advise and help. The development of one's emotional intelligence, followed by the discovery of one's full intelligence profile, is the start of that journey, but even young people should be encouraged to take the next step—the exploration of belief about the purpose of life—because this will start them on the second round of the circle. The natural curiosity of the young is the only fuel needed, provided that it is not damped down. Learning how to learn is, in its essentials, a process of discovering, and then stretching, oneself.

This process, like most of the important things in life, cannot be taught, only encouraged. The lessons learned cannot be graded, because each journey is unique to ourselves. Because small children learn very fast these lessons cannot be postponed until the children go to school. Parents have to be the coaches. That is hard, for the parents are learning too. I once commented that there were three hugely important jobs in society for which neither training nor qualifications were required—those of managers, politicians, and parents.

We have since, in Britain, started to do something about the training of managers instead of assuming that managers were born, not made. Politicians will always escape the competence test, I expect. Parenting, however, is now being taught in a few areas. Some educational authorities in Britain are encouraging parents of children in primary schools to attend discussion groups, and the number of books on good parenting is proliferating. There are even those who would like to see such training becoming a precondition of marriage, but in a free society this will remain a pipe dream.

Although Edward de Bono maintains, convincingly, that we can be taught to think, learning to learn about oneself is more subtle. It does not fit easily into a formal curriculum, but can emerge from the enveloping culture of the school. I once complained to my son's headmaster about what I saw as the excessively academic slant of the school. He replied that because society, and his pupils' parents in particular, regarded examination results as important, he was determined to meet their wishes as efficiently as possible. "But, that done," he said, "we get on with the real education, the individual search for identity and meaning. We all know that that is what we are really about, but we need to get the numbers right first in order to be free to do it."

The underlying lesson there was that real life, and work, has its constraints. We have, most of the time, to operate within those constraints but move beyond them. The challenge for the school is to make up its mind where it wants to go when the constraints have been met. The journey of life is as relevant to the institutions of education as it is to their participants. It is not enough to survive.

7. *Learning is experience understood in tranquillity.*
We learn by reflecting on what has happened. The process seldom works in reverse, although most educational programs assume that it does. We hope that we can teach people how to live before they live, or how to manage before they manage. Little of the teaching sticks. Simulation is the best approximation we can hope for, and where mistakes cannot be allowed it is essential. No one would want an airline pilot to fly before being trained. But no amount of role playing, case studies, or projects can compete with real life. The process of education, therefore, is fundamentally skewed. Most of it comes before, rather than after, experience. We need to build as much experience of reality as we can into schools and universities, but we must also provide more opportunities for reflective learning and requalification after school.

It doesn't end with school or with college. Life itself provides all the learning experiences we need. What is lacking is the time and place and people to help us learn from those experiences. We need to think of the whole educational system as a university of life, in which everyone is entitled to study, sometime, for free, or almost free. This is, in fact, possible in many countries, but it is not presented as a universal right. It should be, particularly as universities and colleges get more modular and globular and virtual, in the process becoming more accessible.

The big danger of a front-loading educational system is that it turns into a one-chance experience. If at first you don't succeed, you don't, usually, try again. That is particularly hard on those whose aptitudes and talents don't fit nicely into the classroom curriculum. In a credential society, where everyone will need a credential or qualification of some sort, an easy-access perpetual college system is essential, and should be made both glamorous and unthreatening.

We should, therefore, be more adventurous in our thinking. I like the idea of a University of the First Age, as pioneered in Birmingham, England, which provides out-of-school experiences and classes for young people. Calling it a university makes it sound respectable, while the work it does is more reality-based and more unconventional than regular classroom studies. I like, too, the notion of a university of the community, in which students are apprenticed to approved non-profit organizations and earn a diploma at the end of a period of successful work, licensing them for similar work elsewhere. Here the college is the work organization and the faculty are the officers of the organization, validated and approved by an outside body. The use of the word "university" confers respectability, while the setting brings reality. The idea of a university for industry, as advocated by the Labour Party in Britain, has some of the same overtones, although it should more properly be a university of *business*, to reflect the idea that it is business, not just industry, that matters today, and that it should be business itself that provides much of the material and the faculty of the university.

We could think more adventurously still and, as part of a universal university of life, endeavor to offer to every young person a mentor from outside the educational system, someone who would take a positive interest in that person's development and progress in life. Mentoring would need to be voluntary or it wouldn't work, and the relationship would have to be acceptable to both parties, but any opportunity for more one-on-one relationships between the generations is worth exploring. Young people lack a variety of adult role models. They meet few adults other than their parents and their teachers, authority figures whom they may well reject in adolescence. It is hard for them to form a realistic view of life ahead from their peer group or the role models of sports or music stars, the only other adults of whom they know anything. The first step to respecting yourself is often to have earned the respect of someone you respect.

One large comprehensive school in London, with 1,450 pupils from 50 different nationalities, has set up a mentoring scheme involving 40 consultants and support staff from a large management consultancy. A visiting executive from another firm was impressed by the early results of this project. "The confidence and aspirations of the students have clearly been increased," he said. Another London school is starting a similar scheme with a neighboring publishing house. More informally, fortunate youngsters have always benefited from the mentorship of family elders, although the advice of strangers tends to be easier to live with than the preachings of relations. If more businesses saw themselves as pools of mentors it is not beyond the bounds of possibility that every teenager could have the option of a volunteer mentor from the world outside. It might be the most useful single thing that business could do to influence the education of our young. It would do no harm to the mentors, either, for teachers often learn more than those they teach.

Change in the Anglo-Saxon tradition comes not by edict but by case law made fashion. There are no sure recipes, only an invitation to create new types of schools for life and work, schools that are appropriate for a new kind of world. It is a world where, more than ever before, we shall each be responsible for our own destiny, our own definition of success, our own journey of discovery.

The danger is that our traditional schools and colleges will lag behind, designed by people from a world that used to be, for a world that will be no more, rather like our armies, which were always well trained for the last war. If we fail, this time, to leap beyond our own experience, we will fail our youth. It is indeed a time for bold imaginings, for reinventing what we understand by education. It is also time to realize that there can be schools in unlikely places, places which we never thought of as schools before. Only in that way will young people acquire the self-confidence that is the prerequisite of self-respect and responsibility.

ELEVEN

A Part for Government

I T I S not enough to promote responsibility and autonomy at work and at school. There is little point in developing the ideas of a full citizenship at work if they do not apply in the wider society. Government has many roles, from the defense of the country to the provision and care of the infrastructure of the land. Here we are only concerned with the part it can and should play in the promotion of individual responsibility, both for oneself and for others.

But first we need to consider the implications of the following fact: capitalism thrives on inequality. Markets separate out the successful from the less successful in a very thorough way. This competitive process creates wealth for the country as a whole, but it doesn't spread it around. Money is like muck, said Francis Bacon, centuries ago—of no use unless it be spread. The responsibility of government is to use some of the riches created by the market, not to make life easy for everyone, but at least to make life possible, not to give away the money but to invest that money, in order to build a decent society. You cannot leave it entirely to those who have the money to do the spreading, because many of them won't, and we have already noted that the money doesn't trickle down or spread itself fast or far enough.

We all want a decent society, and we know that it costs money to build it. Our affluent countries are disfigured by poverty at the edges, by ignorance, anger, and violence. We are creating a generation of thuggish young men who see no place for their muscles in a world of brains and fingertips, or for their macho selves in what will be mainly a service economy. It is hard to see where they can go other than into a world of criminality, or drugs or aimlessness. We can talk of personal responsibility, but without the education or the help to do anything for oneself such talk becomes meaningless for many.

We can each work out that it would pay us all in the long run to have better education for everyone, that help given early to struggling families saves us from spending money later on more police in our cities, more prisons, and more social workers. It is, in a sense, only properly selfish to want a more decent society and to be prepared to pay for it. So why don't we vote for higher taxes? The answer seems to be that we don't trust our governments to spend the money the way we want it spent.

A 1996 study from the Royal Institute of International Affairs in London produced an interesting graph. The richer countries became, the more they saw the state as the servant of the people, instead of the people being the servants of the state. China and Iraq, for example, are down at the bottom, with the state as the master, while the U.S.A., Canada, and Australia, hotly pursued by Germany, France, and the UK, see the state as the servant. The line of argument of this book would suggest that there is an intervening variable here. As we grow accustomed to a little more affluence, we want more control of our own lives and, as a result, want the state to facilitate our life, not to manage it. We want more responsibility. The British will soon formally declare themselves to be "subjects" no longer, but citizens instead.

The thesis of personal responsibility and proper selfishness will be an empty dream for many, unless we can equip them with the resources to achieve some sense of "enough" in material terms and then to go beyond that to reach their goal in life and find their white stone. It is one of the main obligations of government as servant of all its people to make this sort of responsibility a realistic possibility for everyone. This chapter is concerned with how governments might do that, in addition to their other obligations.

A servant government should provide the infrastructure of life, not its superstructure, but should tilt that infrastructure to make it more accessible to those who have fared less well in the market economy or who might do so in future. To build on the infrastructure remains our own personal responsibility. Exercising that responsibility is what gives life its meaning. Any attempt to do it for us is well-meant theft, even if it means that, left to ourselves, we live our lives badly.

The first task must, therefore, be to work out what is meant by the infrastructure of life in a modern society, what should be left to the individual, and how the infrastructure should be tilted. Governments which think it right to control and administer half of a country's annual income themselves have probably got the balance wrong. Restoring a proper balance is likely to be the most important social change in the West in the early years of the next century and will be one change where government has to lead rather than follow.

A servant government must also be under the control of its

citizens if it is to be a proper servant. Information—the right to
know what is going on—involvement—the right to participate in
decisions rather than leave it all to "them"—and individuality—
the right to certain freedoms and protections from that government—are the three essentials of proper citizenship. Governments which say "elect us and leave it to us to act, always, in
your best interests" are turning democracy into elected paternal-
ism or, less generously, into an elected dictatorship.

Responsibility which is exercised once every four or five years
in a polling booth is so minimalist as to be meaningless. Since,
under that system, we can't make much difference in any area,
we might as well not get involved or, if we do, settle for what's
best for us alone, not for the country. Apathy and cynicism are
the real enemies of democracy. By insulating us from any real
responsibility for what happens around us, a paternalistic democracy makes us, literally, careless of others beyond our immediate group. Our ambitions then become too narrowly focused,
selfishness easily becomes improper.

RESTORING THE BALANCE

What counts as the infrastructure? How much should be left to
us, and how much should governments spend on our behalf?

Take some numbers first. In the fifteen countries of the European Union today governments spend between 42 percent and
59 percent of their countries' gross domestic product (GDP). In
America and Japan it is "only" 35 percent. In Singapore and
Hong Kong, countries which are now richer than Britain and
which have longer life expectancy, the take is under 20 percent.
It is the same in the tiger economies of the rest of Asia. Who is
right?

It gets more complicated still. The RIIA study, referred to above, also calculated that the average middle-aged worker in the OECD countries will draw something like $100,000 more in benefits from the state during his or her lifetime than they will have paid in. Their children, however, will have to pay $200,000 to $300,000 more in taxes than they will receive in benefits of one sort or another in the next century. In other words, if we were properly honest, if we weren't borrowing from the next generation, without their knowing it, our governments would be spending even more of our money and, if nothing is done, they will have to spend still more in the future. Should they?

It is not, in the final count, only or even mostly a matter of how much money is required to pay for all the things that are needed, be they our defense forces, our police and prisons, hospitals, schools, roads, sewers, and railways, and, most of all, our pensions, but of who pays it out and therefore has the responsibility for it. By taking that responsibility away from its citizens, governments are implicitly saying that we can't be trusted to look after our own lives. Some suspect that they might be right, that we would be improvident and wouldn't save enough to provide for our old age or for periods out of work, but the danger is that that assumption soon becomes a self-fulfilling prophecy. We become improvident because we don't need to be provident, with the result that the state is left to do it all, while our irresponsibility is encouraged.

Western governments have now realized that they have walked to the edge of a cliff and that if they continue as they are they will fall into a bottomless pit because their promises far exceed their ability to pay. As a result of this economic impasse every government is being forced to return responsibilities to its citizens. The first step backwards from the edge has been to get rid of all the activities which they shouldn't have been doing anyway, running businesses which the private sector could run perfectly well, and usually better. It helped, of course, that the proceeds from this privatization went into the state coffers, reducing the money which they would otherwise have had to borrow or raise from taxes.

The next step is to take the state monopolies of things like water, gas, and electricity supply and sell them off as private monopolies, but regulated by the state. Note the conjuring trick—the customer still pays much the same but the money doesn't go through the government books. Until these private monopolies become true businesses, with competitors who can offer choice to the customer, this form of privatization does little to increase our sense of personal responsibility. The hope is that the lure of gain for the new managers and shareholders will increase the efficiency and the care of the customers—a good start, but not revolutionary enough.

The third step could be more promising, even though it does little to change the government accounts. Take things like health care and education and provide citizens with a mechanism to choose between the different providers, perhaps by giving them something like vouchers, the equivalent of checks signed by the state, for them to spend on the outlet of their choice. The underlying idea is to turn the providers, be they hospitals or schools or universities, into sorts of businesses, so improving their incentives and their efficiency.

I have argued earlier that the concept of businesses in these areas carries unintended consequences, because it allows the providers to choose the customers they want just as much as it allows customers to choose providers. If the providers are sensible business people they will not choose the old, the stupid, or the incurable. It would be better to forget the business angle, but force the providers to compete on standards of service across the board while allowing us all a choice within limits, limits which would need to be both geographical and financial. The sense of responsibility for major decisions in our lives will be fostered.

It is in these areas of health and education that the infrastructure needs tilting, to bring more of the benefits of wealth creation to those who were left out. If we gave bigger vouchers, or their equivalent, to those who need the most—children in inner cities, the chronically ill, the unskilled—these would become the preferred customers because they would carry with them the possibility of more resources.

There are all sorts of practical difficulties with vouchers, but because they encapsulate the idea of choice, they, or something like them, are a prerequisite of responsibility in these areas. There is, we must remember, no point in responsibility if there is no choice. To help the potentially excluded part of the population it is not enough to pour money over them, even by way of investment in schools, hospitals, and the surrounding environment unless the recipients also have an opportunity to exercise some choice and therefore take some responsibility for their own future. As a start, in education, we might offer vouchers for the extracurricular subjects which promote the forms of intelligence not developed in the classroom. We might even consider confining the formal curriculum to the mornings and allowing vouchers to dictate what was done for each young person in the afternoon.

The real revolution comes, however, with the privatization of the welfare and pension systems, which account for nearly half of all government outgoings and can only grow larger as the populations grow older. If nothing changes, for instance, and taxes are kept as they are, the public debt of the U.S.A. in 2030 will be 250 percent of the GDP, twice the level it reached at the end of the Second World War. That won't happen, because it would cost too much money, in interest, to borrow all that, even if anyone were willing to lend it. The situation is no different in Europe, or in Japan. Something has to change: our responsibility for our own future finances.

Go back to those figures for Singapore. The state expenditure figures are low because there is almost nothing in there for pensions or unemployment. That doesn't mean that no one has thought about those things. It is just handled differently. All who work in Singapore contribute to a superannuation fund, normally as much as 40 percent of income, paid jointly by employer and individual. It is the workers' money, invested for them, even if it is mostly invested in government stocks. Contrast Britain, where everyone pays so-called national insurance contributions. These sound the same as the superannuation payments in Singapore, but they aren't. They are effectively an additional income tax which goes straight into the government income stream. Pensions are then paid out of current income.

Most Britons don't realize this. They think that they are building up a nice little pension nest for their old age. They aren't. They will have to rely on the generosity of those who come later, because, as things are, with British pensions linked to the index of prices, not of earnings (earnings normally go up faster), the British state pension in 2030 will be equivalent to only 8 percent of average earnings. Not much to grow fat on. It will be worse for the Germans, and most other Europeans, who are used to looking forward to receiving up to 66 percent of their average lifetime salary, paid out of current government income. When the income isn't there any longer, the pension won't be either.

Government needs to provide the infrastructure for pensions, but not the superstructure. There needs to be a state-regulated and compulsory system whereby a proportion of our earnings, paid partly by ourselves and partly by our employers or our customers, goes straight into a personal pension plan, underwritten by the state. I say customers because the growing number of "portfolio workers" have no employer, only customers. For them, therefore, there has to be a system, like VAT, a value added tax, where a proportion of the sales invoice is automatically handed over to a pension plan, preferably by the customer, as happens in Italy, although there it goes straight into the state coffers. There should also be a compulsory insurance scheme to cover pay during any periods of unemployment. To this can be added the idea of a learning bank, with voluntary contributions matched by employer or government, to be spent on training and education at any stage of the individual's life.

For those who can't pay because they have no earnings for a time or earnings that are too low, there might be a loan scheme, as there will have to be for students in universities, financed by government and to be repaid through the tax system when earnings reach an adequate level. For an unfortunate few, this level may never be reached. They will end their days indebted to the government, a debt written off when they die or reach a certain age. That will be, in practice, no different from the present state of their affairs, but instead of seeing the money they receive as their entitlement they will see it as a loan—a reminder of their responsibility for their own life.

There are no easy solutions to this universal problem. Getting there from here is always going to be technically difficult, expensive—and it will take something like forty years before it is working properly. Which is all the more reason for starting something now. In Britain, all the political parties have begun to think about the problem, which is heartening. In the rest of Europe, and in most of North America, politicians are still hoping that the problem will somehow fail to materialize—at least during their lifetime. Chile, alone of South American countries, has made a start, but their system benefits only those who can afford to pay. Too many are excluded for it to be an adequate answer.

In a sense, all these schemes are merely massaging the statistics because the same amounts of money are involved. Why bother? one might ask. The cynic would say that it would make governments look leaner and fitter, more like Singapore, for example, which takes almost as much money out of its people's pockets but ingeniously routes it differently. Others would argue that it forces the different bodies concerned to be more visible and therefore more likely to be efficient and, possibly, more effective as well. I favor a move in this direction because it emphasizes our personal responsibility for our own lives. We get back what we put in, with interest, we hope. It remains the state's responsibility to create the infrastructure and to see that we use it, and to insure us against system failure, for example, the collapse of the world stock and bond markets in which our money is invested. The state remains the place of last resort when all else fails, but should never be the place of first resort if we are going to have any chance of earning our self-respect.

The danger, however, of such privatized systems is that we think only of ourselves and have no sense of commitment to the larger society. The tax bill is, of course, the outward symbol of that commitment and it is always encouraging to read surveys which record that a majority of people would be prepared to pay higher taxes, in Britain at least, if they could be sure that those taxes would go towards improved education or health care. It is because they can't be sure of where the extra money would end up that they are reluctant to put their votes where their mouth is and vote for a political party that promises to spend more, although this has not recently been put to the test because no political party anywhere is standing on a platform of higher spending. Maybe they should. If the pension money were taken out of the government expenditure figures there would be, by sleight of numbers, apparent room both to reduce taxes *and* to spend more. Our pension contributions, being our money saved for us, would not seem or count as a tax, leaving our taxes to be our contribution to the whole of society.

RESTORING THE WORK

The wealth to be distributed, however, is created by work. Work is also key to a sense of personal responsibility. It remains every country's most serious problem. Lower unemployment figures are deceptive. The reduced numbers of those claiming benefits often mean that people have decided to leave the workforce early. This is not good news. People need to stay in the wage economy as long as possible, both to give them enough to live on and to reduce the burden on the next generation. The work, therefore, has to be good work, paying a living wage and providing some sense of personal worth. If it does neither of these things society will continue to get more unequal and more people will feel cheated of a life.

If governments could wave their wand and create jobs for all, many of their budgetary and other problems would be solved. If only it were that easy. Some of it might be. If governments were not so fixated by efficiency in the non-competitive areas of the infrastructure, and if they could define extra expenditure in, for example, schools and hospitals, as a form of investment not as a current cost, they could create more jobs in and around those places. This would make the schools and hospitals less efficient in terms of costs, maybe, but more effective in output.

I once suggested to the South Africans that they should con-

sider adopting what was then the Japanese solution to employment. The Japanese differentiated, either by design or by historical precedent, between the competitive export businesses and
the non-competitive sectors of the domestic economy which
were heavily regulated. Their department stores were obviously
overstaffed, with assistants to greet you at the door and to press
the elevator buttons for you. When I was last there, buying a
railway ticket in Tokyo's central station required a sequence of
transactions at different windows, behind each of which sat a
person. As the Japanese deregulate their domestic economy in
order to revive the general economy there will be fewer of these
extra people, but the principle that it was better to pay people for
working rather than for doing nothing, as long as it did not hurt
one's exports, seemed to me to be a sensible one.

Where industries are internationally competitive, efficiency
and effectiveness are both essential. Jobs should be kept to a
minimum and only the best people should be on the payroll. But
in the non-competitive areas of government, most of which are
people intensive, the South Africans could, I suggested, relax the
criteria and employ more people than were technically needed.
It would be no more expensive than paying them not to work; the
extra people could improve the care and attention given to the
users and would, themselves, learn by working, particularly if
proper training was provided.

Other countries could do the same. It would be a way of
tilting the infrastructure towards those who need to be involved.
The real scope for more work, however, lies in the infinitely
expandable market for personal services, be they in the areas of
caring for young and for old, of help in the house or the garden,
of part-time work in stores and shops, or of part-time professional assistance to individuals or institutions. Nearly half of the
workforce is already either part-time or self-employed, and it will

be this section of the workforce that will provide the opportunities for more and more of us in the future. But this sector is, by its nature, insecure. It is also hard for many to penetrate because they have to sell themselves and their services—not something that most of us find easy.

There is scope here for what Geoff Mulgan and Tom Bentley of the think tank Demos have termed employee mutuals. These are intermediate organizations which employ labor but subcontract it. They are employee agencies of a sort, except that they work for the individual, who is a co-owner of the mutual, as well as for the end customer. The mutuals would offer the individual training, would act as his or her marketing agent, collect monies on their behalf and, in general, act as their home base, a refuge in a difficult world. The organization would be financed by a levy on the pay earned by each individual, but any overall surplus would belong to its members. Government help would be required to devise a new legal form for these mutuals, a tax structure, and some assistance with a few pilot models. That sort of help would be a modest investment in the infrastructure of work, directed towards those who need it most, but leaving them with the responsibility for their own lives.

I have, in the past, suggested that these employee mutuals offered a possible new role for trade unions. Sadly, the unions are still locked into their role as the protectors of permanent employees. The option is still open and would be welcomed by many. Organizations used to provide the means for most of us to connect ourselves with the market, to turn our skills and our time into useful goods and services. Nowadays, more and more of us are going to have to do it for ourselves. If work has, to a large degree, moved outside the large organizations so, I believe, should the organizations created to protect those workers.

RE-INVENTING DEMOCRACY

Thus far we have only suggested rearranging the tax structure so that fewer of our payments go through government hands, leaving us with more sense of responsibility for our own lives, even though we are paying out the same money. I now want to suggest that we should take seriously the expressed willingness of most people to pay more tax if it made a more civilized society, and if they had more confidence in the results of their expenditure.

More taxes will be acceptable, I suggest, if they are locally voted and locally spent. If we can watch the local environment improving, can feel proud again of the schools and hospitals in our neighborhood, then and only then will we feel that our taxes have been spent as we wanted. And if things don't improve, we know who was responsible and can remove them from office. Democracy can still work, if it is local.

I am also a convert to the idea of hypothecated or earmarked taxes. No government likes such taxes because they bind their hands, requiring them to spend the tax on what it has been collected for, and to show how it has been spent. The reluctance is understandable but, once again, efficiency needs to be tempered by effectiveness. If we paid a separate health tax we would feel that it was more like an insurance than a tax and would understand better what health care costs. Similarly with education. There would inevitably be those who would want to opt out of the taxes, claiming that they wanted to make their own provision, or that they had no children to be educated, but their contributions could and should be presented as their stake in an inclusive society—the cost of citizenship in a decent world. It might happen, however, that we would turn out to be willing to spend more on health and education if we were sure that that was where the money was going to end up.

These earmarked taxes would need to be graduated as income tax is now, but by removing health, education, and pensions from the general budget, governments would be able to eliminate income tax for all but the richest citizens. Income tax, seen as a tax on labor, has always been resented and has always added to the cost of that labor. Removing most of it and relying for general income on expenditure taxes of varying sorts would encourage people to work more, even for modest wages, and to save more because only expenditure would be taxed.

Expenditure taxes are regressive. That is, they penalize the poor disproportionately. It would be important, therefore, either to introduce something like a basic income, given as a right to everyone, which would be complicated and expensive; or, more interestingly, to subsidize essential products rather than their consumers. At first sight this would seem to be in contradiction to the best free market practices, but there is no reason why a competitive market should not operate underneath the subsidy levels.

Were this principle to be applied to public housing, public transport, basic foodstuffs, and utilities, it would mean that people on low pay could still get by, and that any extra money would be a sort of riches, because it would not be needed for essentials. In other words, the level of material "enough" would come down, freeing more people to define their lives the way they wanted to. Since these services would also be available at reduced cost to the more affluent whose taxes had paid for the subsidies, there would be an obvious and direct relationship with their taxes. Instead of supplementing the income of the lower paid, as most countries do now, we could cut the cost of essentials, thereby making existence possible without apparent subsidy and giving people back their dignity.

The subsidy may not be apparent, but some will argue it is already there in places, and can distort the market mechanism. Yet we don't call it subsidy when we offer health care or education apparently for free. When the British Museum announces that it will not impose entrance charges on anyone, no one talks of market distortion. Taxes spent on cost reduction for essentials can be precisely monitored, are visible to all, reduce the cost of living and therefore of wages, and reduce or even eliminate the poverty trap involved in subsidizing income.

The best way to encourage more initiatives in looking for work has to be to increase the immediate rewards of finding that work. The elimination of income tax combined with the reduction in the cost of essentials would go a long way towards doing just that. As importantly, individuals would retain the responsibility for their own lives rather than being so obviously dependent on the state.

THE STRUCTURES OF INVOLVEMENT

In 1996 the roads of France were blocked by trucks. They brought that side of Europe to a halt. It was a very French form of public protest, copied from the farmers who have often taken their tractors to the streets to express their anger or frustration. This time it was the truck drivers, looking, on the face of it, for more money, shorter working weeks, and earlier retirement, but to Theodore Zeldin, the social historian, it was another sign of the changing face of politics in Europe. The truck drivers, he said, were looking for dignity and respect as much as for better terms and conditions. This search for personal dignity will begin to transform politics as groups of people as diverse as students and doctors, teachers and judges complain that you cannot educate people to be free and responsible and then treat them as if they were passive instruments of the state, telling them what and how to teach, what drugs to prescribe, as in France, or what punishments to deal out in court, as in Britain.

A generation ago the drivers would not have complained about their jobs the way they did in 1996. In those times the world of the industrial revolution still operated. What mattered was to keep the factory busy, and people were hired to do just that. If the work was boring, dirty, or mundane, well, that was the way it was. People moaned but accepted this. Jobs are different now. They are supposed to be interesting and varied, to allow people room to exercise their discretion and to grow their talents. Money is not enough, today. Personal dignity matters too. Jobs must first suit their people and then be profitable.

A servant government has to be seen to be working for its citizens, with their consent and agreement, not ordering them about for its convenience. If we are to feel that it is our government serving us, we need to be kept informed, encouraged to participate where appropriate, and be assured that we as individuals will be guaranteed our basic freedoms. While it may often be necessary to remind people that rights entail obligations, it is also pertinent to remind our rulers, who should be our servants, that obligations need to be balanced by rights, because it is rights that buttress dignity.

The first duty of a government, therefore, is to inform its people. It is, however, the assumption of most people in authority that the truth is too important, or too complicated, to be entrusted to ordinary folk. Sometimes this is true; in war, for instance, or in a national emergency. More often it is an excuse because explanations are too difficult or too painful. If, however, governments truly see themselves as the servants of the people they should accept the necessity of something akin to the open-book management described in Chapter Nine and tell the people everything—well, almost everything. Secrets evaporate when exposed to the light and then we mostly wonder why they were ever secret.

It is for this reason that I have also become a convert to the idea of referenda. It is argued that the decisions reached by this method are often wrong. But there is little evidence that they are any worse than those taken on the people's behalf by their elected representatives. Those countries with extensive experience of referenda find that the necessity for a referendum forces politicians to explain the issues. At the same time the populace is encouraged to focus their minds on the questions before them. Referenda make the symbolic point that some decisions are too important to be left to politicians, and that the people can be trusted to be responsible for their own future as a society. Referenda are a form of public education and for that reason alone we need more of them.

Technology will help. When we can push a button, after inserting our identification into the computer, and no longer have to line up in the rain outside a commandeered schoolhouse in order to vote, we shall find referenda an appealing prospect. They have worked well in Switzerland for 130 years, with citizens able to challenge government decisions at each level of government, and even to put forward their own proposals if they can collect enough supporting signatures.

In California referenda complicate the task of government with what look like irresponsible decisions by the majority of citizens. Maybe democracy by referenda has to be learned by long and hard experience. It is the democracy of mature states.

That we shall get more referenda, however, seems certain as the electorate flexes its muscles, wanting to take responsibility for the more important decisions of the age. It will be more referenda or the alternatives, more pressure group politics, more demonstrations, and more barricades. Referenda seem more civilized, even if they are more boring.

Citizen juries, particularly where local issues are concerned, are another structure for information. Open hearings, with official witnesses appearing in front of fellow citizens to argue their point of view, provide an opportunity for those who wish to get involved, for others to watch or listen, and for officials to have a chance, indeed an obligation, to inform and educate ordinary people about the issues. We shall see more of these, too, because they are one aspect of subsidiarity.

Subsidiarity is the principle that decisions and responsibilities should lie as low down in the system as is possible. To make it work, the holders of the responsibilities, the repositories of subsidiarity if you like, have to be educated up to their responsibilities. You can't, responsibly, give responsibility to incompetents. On the other hand, those people will remain incompetent unless they have the incentive of responsibility. It has to be a chicken and egg process, in step and by degrees. Citizen juries are one way into the process, but they are of no use if they are only cosmetic. Power has to be truly devolved if people are going to be committed to local decisions.

Devolution looks to be inevitable—fortunately, in my view. A more prosperous and educated population wants more choice and more room to be different if they want to. Uniformity allows for too little of either. Yet a centralized government can only manage through uniformity. Uniformity stifles individuality and responsibility and it is for that reason that people will, in the end, pull power back to themselves.

Fukuyama predicts that at "the end of history" the combination of democracy and capitalism means that voters will be like dogs lying on their backs in the sun, waiting to be tickled and fed. There will be no great causes anymore, or things worth dying for.

Maybe, but there are many smaller private and local causes. Politics will increasingly be about the small things of life, not the bigger things. This is not necessarily bad or sad. The equality which uniformity sought to provide by law and regulation has in fact begun to happen. It has happened more informally as men and women start to do more things for themselves locally, empowering themselves and, as a result, treating each other in private and locally with more respect.

The middle layers are disappearing, not just in businesses and organizations, but everywhere. Technology is the driver. So much of life's hierarchies are determined by information. If you don't know what your blood pressure is or what the danger levels are when you do know, then you have to ask the doctor. But if you have this information at your fingertips, then the doctor is there only to deal with the bad news, if there is any. As the information age gets underway, with so much of what we need to know literally at our fingertips and on our television screens, we will be able to buy and sell our own houses without the aid of lawyers, arrange our own holidays and travel without the help of travel agencies, buy and sell our own shares without any stockbroker, vote without leaving our home, and educate ourselves and our children wherever we please, without the help of teachers.

We can do most of this already, of course, but it will become much easier as the information providers get their act together and as computers and their successors become more user-friendly. We won't want to abandon the human side of things entirely, but the role of the middle layers, the professionals, will change from information providers to interpreters, mentors, and coaches. We will then, inevitably, decide more things for ourselves because it will be easier, in this "press, choose, and press again" sort of world. In the process we will learn, and as we learn we will develop our self-confidence. Once we have learned to decide more things for ourselves we will be reluctant to allow others to decide things for us.

There will, therefore, be a split in politics, with the really big issues being decided, whether we like it or not, beyond the boundaries of the nation-state, either by the pressures of the global markets or by economic and military alliances such as the European Union, NATO, or their equivalents, while the smaller, but to many people, more important issues of roads and schools, police and hospitals, will be regional decisions, taken more locally by locals. The nation-state may, in the long term, turn out to be one of those middle layers which disappears unless it is already, in reality, more like a region, as countries like Ireland and the Netherlands arguably are.

From my point of view this is mostly good news, because it allows individuals to become more involved with the things that matter most to them. They will be more in charge of the decisions of their personal lives and more able to have a voice in the affairs of their region. Responsibility, both for themselves and for those around them, will be enhanced. Self-respect will grow, as a result of that enlarged responsibility, and with self-respect a greater tolerance for others' rights and ways. Society should gradually become less angry. Proper selfishness will have prevailed.

The end point of the journey may be desirable, but getting there won't be easy. Governments will twist and turn in their efforts to keep control. Professionals of all types will resist the change in their status from being the guardians of knowledge to being counselors and interpreters. There will be the temptation to make things more complicated than they need be in order to retain the need for the expert. We will all take some time to realize that we can do more for ourselves than we had thought. But just as do-it-yourself took off in the home improvement area once technology made it easier, so it is likely to be in the information area.

We will, however, feel naked at times, bewildered by a surplus of information and by the complexity of much of life. If we are to be free to experiment with this new extended responsibility, there has to be a bottom line of personal security. For that reason, America has its constitution and a Supreme Court to protect the individual rights enshrined in it. We need to have our rights printed large and clear so that we can more boldly exercise our responsibility. Responsibility is born of rights, not the other way round, and responsibility remains the essential key to a truly proper selfishness.

An Epilogue

THE WORLD IN 2097

Country Life, the British journal of the countryside, celebrated its centenary in 1997 in some style. They got headlines for their photograph of a lady wearing nothing but her pearls (so tastefully done that few would have noticed anything unusual), but they also distributed a copy of their first edition, dated 8 January 1897, and commissioned a book called *A Vision of the Country A.D. 2097*, edited by the economist and environmentalist David Fleming.

The combination of past, present, and future, spanning two hundred years, is unusual outside the fantasies of science fiction. *Country Life* admits that this particular fantasy makes for uncomfortable reading. People will be eating algae when conventional food sources fail to cope with a doubling of the world's population. They will watch athletic ninety-year-olds competing at the Gera-Olympics. Yorkshire might become the British Provence because of climate change; our summers will be too hot and the sun too dangerous, but our winters will be more severe.

The rich will be very rich. Global communications and a global economy will bring global fortunes to those few who can succeed in a fiercely competitive world. It is a world in which the best are everywhere and the rest are nowhere. Since much of this money will be generated in cyberspace it will be difficult to tax. The state will not, therefore, be able to support the growing numbers of old and unemployed beyond the most basic of subsistence levels. The bands of the dispossessed will wander the land like the beggars of Elizabethan England, threatening the private oases which the very rich will create for themselves, protected by their private armies. Democracy may crack under the strain, giving way to new systems of power and patronage where the rich decide on behalf of the rest. Offices won't be needed and cities will crumble into urban wastelands.

We have seen the future according to *Country Life* and it is the Middle Ages. It is tempting to dismiss it all as fiction. After all, looking back at that first edition of one hundred years ago, the changes are not as dramatically different as the future is assumed to be. There have been social and technological developments, certainly, but in spite of two disastrous world wars most of Britain is better off and its citizens at least as happy as they were.

To think that way would be dangerously complacent. Change may not be as violent as a world war but demography, climate, and environmental decay can be much more potent although less obvious, because they creep rather than erupt. The global market is not going to be a comfortable place. The sorting of the business wheat from the chaff will be much more brutal, and any talk of national sovereignty is futile in the borderless world of cyberspace.

As I write, the people of Tirana and Seoul are raging on the streets because uncontrolled capitalism has robbed them of their rights and of their savings. Next year it will be somewhere else. Maastricht has become a dirty word in much of Europe as countries cut their public spending to meet its arbitrary criteria. In Paris and Rome—and maybe yet in Bonn and London—the crowds gather to demonstrate their anger at the rule of the money men. In the post-Soviet world of Russia and the old Soviet Republics carpetbaggers and mafiosi steal the riches that were once supposed to be the property of the people. In the Valley of the Sun, in Arizona, Mexicans work sixteen-hour days for five dollars an hour or less, peanuts in a world of affluence. How long before they and their fellows rebel against the inequity of a system which grows richer as they grow poorer and calls it productivity?

Equality for all turned out to mean poverty for all. Now liberty for all means riches only for some. The French are right—only fraternity can link those two opposites of liberty and equality, but fraternity too seems in short supply. To restore the balance between the freedom to be ourselves and the need for a decent society around us, we need to combine a concern for ourselves in a dangerous and uncertain world with a due regard for the needs of others—a proper selfishness. We cannot legislate for that, only hope that more people see the sense in it.

THE GOOD NEWS

The future is not all gloom. Perhaps economic growth and the "cultivation" which Adam Smith thought should be the proper

purpose of society are no longer incompatible. One pleasing outcome of the information age is that more of us can enjoy the
good things which life can offer without spoiling the world for
everyone else. There are some interesting possibilities on the
horizon.

1. Many of the things for which we will be shopping in
   future use up much less of our environment. A CD-
   ROM, for example, which can contain on one disc all of
   the Encyclopedia Britannica, leaves the forests un-
   touched, takes up less shelf space in the shops, needs
   no sweatshops to produce it, and no huge trucks to
   transport it. Many of the consumer goods of the information age are as environmentally neutral as the computer disc—you only have to be careful that you don't
   get a backache from sitting too long in front of your
   screen, cruising on the Internet.

2. There again, the new age fashions will help. The new
   growth areas include the health business—not healing
   but keeping healthy, through exercise, sport, walking,
   and cycling—all environmentally friendly activities as
   well as being good for both mind and body. To the
   health business we can add education, not the educational drilling we received as children but the enriching
   education of adulthood when we choose what we learn
   and where we learn. Half of the students in higher education are now "mature," over age twenty-five, and the
   proportion will surely grow. If some of the buildings of
   this education business still look ugly, we should not
   despair—much of the learning can now take place anywhere, in groups of any size, thanks to the new technol-

ogies. Less travel and more of the cultivation that Adam Smith wanted.

3. Health and education are the two most prominent examples of the new scene in economics. As we get richer we spend more of our money on time than on things: time to invest in our own lives; time to learn; time to walk, talk, and eat with friends; time to travel and time to read; time to go to theaters, cinemas, and concerts as well as race tracks and bingo halls—all cultivation of a sort. Time, also, to sit and watch the square box in the living room or the bedroom, which may not always be "cultivation" of the highest order, but at least it keeps us off the streets and out of our cars. Before long, too, that square box will become the information center of the home, an essential interactive piece of equipment, no longer merely passive entertainment or wallpaper sound.

4. Who, one might ask, will have the time to spend all their money on time? Many more people, is the answer, as more and more of us become members of the Third Age, that chunk of life beyond full-time work and parenting. As we live longer and as work lives shorten, the Third Age stretches from about fifty-five to, with luck, eighty or beyond. By the end of this century one third of the adult population of the West will be in this Third Age. These twenty-five years can, if we are sensible and plan for them, be very productive years, but they will not be years when we try to accumulate more "things." This is a slimming-down time of life, a time for being more than for getting, a chance to catch up on all the things we wish that we had done or seen or

been in earlier years. With luck and good medicine we shall be healthy, able to enjoy all the "time products" we can buy, and with better financial planning in our earlier years, more of us could have the money to spend.

5. There will, however, never be enough of this Third Age money, because for most of us the Second Age of work will have been too short and our savings too frugal to cover twenty-five years of income-less retirement. We shall both need and want to do some work. That work, however, will most often be advising or caring in one way or another, or it will be helping out, doing some part-time work in the service sector. Such work can add great value but leaves no clutter. More people contributing some of their wisdom, time, and experience either as consultants to businesses or as para-professionals in schools, hospitals, welfare organizations, and churches, create economic growth both through their earnings and by the value added.

6. People are more adaptable than we give them credit for. I was recently given the opportunity to travel around Britain interviewing, for a radio series, some twenty-five assorted individuals who were selected as a reasonable cross-section of people working in the so-called new age of work. There were portfolio workers, telecommuters, people who had started their own businesses after redundancy, dual career couples with children, individuals in the heart of the knowledge organizations (consultancy, finance, and advertising), a househusband and two unemployed men, as well as a group of fifteen-year-olds at a normal country school. The adults were all

living lives that they had never planned on. They had had to adapt to both unexpected success (the chief executive of the large advertising agency was only thirty-two and already at the top of his career) and to unexpected shock.

With the exception of the two unemployed men, for whom life seemed pointless and hopeless, they had all taken the changes in their stride and were, it seemed to me, relieved that the responsibility for their futures was now so clearly in their own hands. "I'm pleased to say that I'm unemployable now," one man said, meaning that he would never want to work inside an organization again. Similarly, the children seemed to be under no illusions about the world that awaited them outside the school gates and were quite determined that they would be in charge of their own lives, even if they contracted some part of those lives, for a time, to an organization.

7. Success has many faces. Asked how they defined success, none of that group, not even the unemployed, spoke of money. They talked of doing something they felt good about, of their families and their hopes for them, which were not particularly monetary, of being able to make the most of their own potential. Of course, although they were intended to be representative of our new society, they may not have been, and they may not have told me the whole truth, but what they did say, all of them, was that the world they saw made up in its opportunities for all its extra problems. They had not fallen victim to the fallacy of the single criterion, the idea that there is only one measuring stick for a life. Each one of us can be successful in a different way.

Those seven trends and indicators suggest that we now have the chance to achieve what Adam Smith, in a pessimistic mood, thought impossible: to enjoy both growth *and* cultivation. Shopping malls will, no doubt, remain the favorite congregating places for a while and our roads will still be crowded, but the malls may have more spaces for eating, meeting, and greeting than just for shopping and the roads more tracks for cyclists and walkers as well as cars. The gym looks set to replace the church as the center of the community, although members worship the body, not the deity. Who knows, in fact, what may happen when more of us need fewer things, when there is more time to sit and think, more chance to be something other than just an "employee" or "customer," the only words that used to matter in yesterday's economics.

THE ENTREPRENEURIAL IMPERATIVE

If we want to see more of the good news than the bad we will have to do it for ourselves. It is no good waiting for some unidentified "they" to fix our world for us. Thomas Jefferson argued that good economics should promote good citizenship. He was worried, then, about the drift away from agriculture and the care of one's own plot, into impersonal businesses. No longer, he feared, would we take responsibility for ourselves and those around us once we were cogs in someone else's machine. Maybe economics is once again forcing us back into the care of our own plot, although it is often now a "virtual" plot, consisting of resources within oneself rather than outside the window. One British study records that 40 percent of those leaving the welfare registers are starting their own businesses. Whether this is led by desperation

or by a new entrepreneurial urge in society, it is one sign of a
growing realization that things start with us.

Others are increasingly turning their entrepreneurial skills
to help the less fortunate. Take the story of Helen Taylor-
Thompson and the Mildmay Mission Hospital in Shoreditch,
east London. In 1982 the Mildmay, a district general hospital,
was due to close. Helen Taylor-Thompson, who had been involved with the hospital for thirty years, was determined that it
would not shut. After a long campaign she persuaded the government to allow the hospital to reopen by leaving the National
Health Service and leasing the buildings on a peppercorn rent.

Before long the Mildmay had become one of the leading centers for AIDS care, with an international reputation for innovation. In 1988 it became the first AIDS hospice in Europe. It has
thirty-two suites for the terminal care of people with AIDS,
housed in the old Victorian hospital. In addition it has a facility
especially built to treat parents with AIDS, without separating
them from their children. This year it plans to open a treatment
center in Kampala, Uganda. Mildmay is a world class institution
created from a hospital that was regarded as worthless fifteen
years ago, born out of the entrepreneurial energy of one woman.

This story is one of a number recounted by Charles Leadbetter in *The Rise of the Social Entrepreneur*. He argues that the
British tradition of welfare must not be abandoned, but it must
be changed. Social entrepreneurs are the harbingers of that
change, devising new ways to provide support and development
for those excluded from the opportunities of the new society. A
project to create two thousand social entrepreneurs before the
year 2000 *("2,000 for 2000")* is planned in Britain, as is a School
of Social Entrepreneuring, which would have to be as unlike a
traditional school as possible, because no one ever learned to be
an entrepreneur in a classroom.

In Britain in 1996, two women, uninvited, captured the emotions of the people and forced a government to change the law. Frances Lawrence, the widow of a schoolteacher knifed to death by a teenager in the street outside his school, launched an appeal for a moral revival and a ban on knives. Similarly, Ann Pearston, a member of the Dunblane community where sixteen small children and their teacher were gunned down in their school by a man with a handgun, launched a campaign to have handguns banned, an appeal which found universal approval and brought about a change in the law. Asked to vote for their Personality of the Year in 1996, the listeners of the BBC's "Today" program voted these two women onto their short list, along with Aung San Suu Kyi, the Burmese dissident—three women who have each changed the world a bit, on their own initiative.

In America, another woman won admiration for a similar display of courage in adversity, which became a determination to change the way things were. Carolyn McCarthy's husband was killed in the Long Island Railroad massacre, whereupon she successfully ran for Congress as a popular grassroots candidate favoring tighter gun control. It may be no accident that it is women who are often the first ones to point out the absurdities and obscenities of our modern world, for their sensitivities are more attuned to the paradoxes endemic in our idea of progress, but we have to admire those who do not stop at pointing them out but who are entrepreneurial enough to try to do something about it.

Such people are examples of proper selfishness at its best, because entrepreneurs, whether social or commercial, often discover aspects of themselves in the pursuit of something beyond themselves. Such people are not content to let the status quo be the way forward. They itch to make a difference. We should encourage them. More than half of the new start-ups in the service sector businesses in both Europe and America are the work of women. Often these women have honed their skills in the larger corporations only to find their ambitions checked by the so-called "glass ceiling." Almost accidentally, the corporations have become the nurseries for frustrated entrepreneurs. They should turn this to positive account and do it more deliberately, in the hope that they can retain some of the best for themselves, including some women, while seeding the community with the others. The workplace has always been the real school for life. Perhaps it just needs to change its curriculum a little to tune in with the new age of personal initiative.

THE GREATEST PAINTING
IN THE WORLD

I have no hesitation in naming what is for me the greatest painting in the world. It is the *Resurrection* by Piero della Francesca. It is still where it was painted more than five hundred years ago, on the wall in the town hall of Borgo San Sepolcro, a small town. We should be thankful that frescoes are so very difficult to move, because it remains a thrill to make the journey across the Italian hills to that small town, to walk into the room where Piero painted, and to see before you what he did there for his fellow citizens.

The painting is large; it fills the wall. It depicts Christ rising from the tomb, while the soldiers, who were supposed to be guarding it, sleep on, slumped against the side of the stone tomb. The figure of Christ is noble, imposing, set against the grey light of early morning in an Umbrian setting of hills and cypresses. It is the eyes that strike you first, piercing, bold, purposeful, hard to escape from. This is the face of a man who sees life whole and knows his place in it. I have stood and watched that painting for long, long spells and have always come away disturbed and yet invigorated.

Everyone draws his or her own message from great art. For me the *Resurrection* carries a metaphorical meaning rather than a conventional religious one. I am free, goes that message, to break free from my past and to recreate myself. If I do so, I will be stronger and more sure. Even if my life up to now is counted a failure by many, as was the life of the man in that painting, the best is yet to come. I do not have to stay slumped and sleeping like those soldiers, waiting for my orders. It may be that I shall not see the full results of my efforts, but I should so strive that others may profit, even if it be after my death. That is the sort of immortality that I can understand. It is a message that applies to all people, and to all businesses and institutions. The best is always yet to come if we can rise from our past.

It is that hope which sustains me, that and the certainty that we are most fully ourselves when we lose ourselves in our concern for others, or in a cause that is greater than we are. We were wrong to have put our faith in an undiluted ideology of self-interest when we should have trusted our humanity more than the system. We can override that system, just as we can override the programming of nature. We should trust ourselves to be both great and good, and if sometimes that trust is misplaced, more often it will be merited, for there is that within all of us which cries out for a better and a fairer world. Where better to start than where we are?

Bibliography

Listed below are the principal authors to whom I refer in the text, along with others who, although not directly mentioned, have been an important influence on my thinking.

d'Ancona, Matthew. *The Ties That Bind Us.* London; The Social Market Foundation, 1996.

Bauman, Zygmunt. *Alone Again.* London: Demos, 1994.

Bennis, Warren, and Patricia Ward Biederman. *Organizing Genius.* Reading, Mass.: Addison-Wesley, 1997.

Branden, Nathaniel. *Taking Responsibility.* New York: Simon and Schuster, 1996.

Case, John. *Open Book Management.* New York: HarperCollins, 1995.

Collins, James C., and Jerry I. Porras. *Built to Last.* New York: Harper Business, 1994.

Damasio, A. *Descartes' Error.* London: Picador, 1995.

Davidson, James Dale, and William Rees-Mogg. *The Sovereign Individual*. London: Macmillan, 1997.

Dawkins, Richard. *The Blind Watchmaker*. London: Penguin, 1993.

Drucker, Peter. *Post-Capitalist Society*. Oxford: Butterworth Heinemann, 1993.

Fukuyama, Francis. *Trust*. New York: The Free Press, 1995.

Gardner, Howard, *Frames of Mind*. London: Heinemann, 1983.

Goleman, Daniel. *Emotional Intelligence*. London: Bloomsbury, 1996.

Goyder, George. *The Just Enterprise*. London: The Adamantine Press, 1993.

Hampden-Turner, Charles. *The Seven Cultures of Capitalism*. New York: Currency Doubleday, 1993.

Hillman, James. *The Soul's Code*. New York: Random House, 1996.

Hirsch, Fred, and Paul Kegan. *The Social Limits to Growth*. London: Routledge, 1997.

Huntington, Samuel. *The Clash of Civilizations*. New York: Simon and Schuster, 1996.

Jones, Barry. *Sleepers, Wake!*. Melbourne: Oxford University Press, 1996.

Kay, John, in *Prospect*, London, May 1996

Kinsman, Francis. *Millennium*. London: W. H. Allen, 1989.

Korten, David C.. *When Corporations Rule the World*. San Francisco: Brett-Koehler, 1995.

Kuttner, Robert. *Everything for Sale*. New York: Knopf, 1997.

Leadbetter, Charles. *The Rise of the Social Entrepreneur*. London: Demos, 1997.

Mohn, Reinhard. *Success Through Partnership*. New York: Doubleday, 1986.

Moore, Thomas. *Care of the Soul.* New York: HarperCollins, 1992.

Mulgan, Geoff. *Connexity.* London: Chatto and Windus, 1997.

Novak, Michael. *Business as a Calling.* New York: The Free Press, 1996.

Ormerod, Paul. *The Death of Economics.* London: Faber, 1994.

Orwell, George, *Keep the Aspidistra Flying.* London: Penguin, 1936.

Plender, John. *A Stake in the Future.* London: Nicholas Brealey, 1997.

Putnam, Robert. *Making Democracy Work.* Princeton University Press, 1993.

Ridley, Matt. *The Origins of Virtue.* London: Viking, 1996.

Secretan, Lance H.K.. *Reclaiming Higher Ground.* Toronto: Macmillan, 1996.

Singer, Peter. *How Are We to Live?.* Melbourne: Mandarin, 1995.

Thuillier, P. *The Great Implosion.* Quoted by Julia Rosetti in *Resurgence,* No. 180 (January–February 1997).

Thurow, Lester. *The Future of Capitalism.* London: Nicholas Brealey, 1996.

Wheatley, Margaret J. and Myron Kellner-Rogers. *A Simpler Way.* San Francisco: Brett-Koehler, 1996.

Whyte, David. *The Heart Aroused.* New York: Currency Doubleday, 1994.

Zeldin, Theodore. *An Intimate History of Humanity.* London: Sinclair-Stevenson, 1994.

Index

Printed in the United States
by Baker & Taylor Publisher Services